SOUTHERN BRANCH LINES

Frontispiece

One picture that says it all, the railway booking hall as seen until the sixties, little changed from when the railway was built. The timber structure of the South Eastern Railway at Elmers End, junction for two branch lines, as seen in B.R. days. The floor has been sprinkled with a mixture of water and disinfectant and swept. Around the walls are the standard notices of the time including the fog service, a greatly reduced service operated at short notice during the era of the great fogs of the fifties and sixties. The diminutive bookstall has its own gas supply, the station being entirely gas lit; and the entrance door to the platform has no handle—this prevented commuters from gaining access to the platform when trains were leaving. The door would be locked by the ticket collector as the train left in the morning rush hour. In the days before concrete and plastics, timber was the cheap material. Photograph taken on 22 March 1960.

SOUTHERN BRANCH LINES

by C.J. Gammell

G.R.Q. PUBLICATIONS

ISBN 0 946863 0 24
Typeset by Pace Photosetting,
Hemel Hempstead
Printed and bound in Great Britain
by Bocardo Press Ltd., Oxford.

Published by
G.R.Q. Publications
43F Anerley Park
London SE20 8NQ

CONTENTS

	page
Branch Lines in South London	8
Branch Lines to The South West of London	18
Branch Lines in Kent	23
Branch Lines in Surrey & Sussex	42
Branch Lines in Hampshire	55
Branch Lines in The Isle of Wight	65
Branch Lines in Wilts, Somerset & Dorset	72
Branch Lines in Devon & Cornwall	79
Acknowledgements	94
Bibliography, Appendix	95
Index	96

The Southern halt had many standardised features and all components were made to a specification for a catalogue; the concrete components were made at Exmouth Junction engineers depot. The platform sections, fencing and nameboard parts could be seen throughout the system. Yarde Halt on the Torrington to Halwill line was only one coach length long.

A unique event occurred on 6 August 1956 when AIX class DS 377 , the Brighton Works shunter, in Stroudley livery, worked the Centenary special on the Caterham branch. The AIX is seen here in Purley goods yard.

The Southern Railway 1923 to 1947 and its successor the Southern Region was one of the most remarkable railway systems ever to exist. The railway systems in Britain had been grouped in 1923 to form four large railways, and the Southern, by way of its geographical location, was the odd one out. The three other railways carried the nation's freight, connected the principle cities of the country with the capital and served the industrial heartland of the Midlands, North, and Wales. The Southern was a passenger-carrying railway but had an enormous variety of traffic. There were the international trains to the Continent, elegant pullman services, and the boat trains up from Britain's premier passenger port at Southampton.

The Southern had the World's largest suburban electrified system and electrification was a policy that the management pursued with the utmost vigour. Over the electrified network, steam trains to the outer reaches of the railway intermingled with fast electric expresses. Southern locomotives were built for power and rapid acceleration—for this very reason the railway built the sturdy Maunsell designs and the unique Bulleid pacifics. It was to the Southern that the L.M.S. came for a powerful express locomotive design when Derby were incapable of building one, and it was North British who supplied them off the peg. Today, Maunsell engines are still at work—a testimony to the soundness of the design.

The Southern had a well organised engineering department which produced all the necessary buildings required from a catalogue of standardised parts from a lamp-post to a complete station. The ballast was provided for the entire system from one railway owned quarry in the West of England. The railway never threw anything away, and redundant locomotives and rolling stock from electrified lines became transferred to other parts of the system. The Isle of Wight flourished on London & South Western Railway engines and South Eastern & Chatham, and London, Brighton & South Coast coaches.

The Southern, apart from creating its own charisma of green and white notices and nameboards, green coaches, engines and stations, had an extremely energetic publicity department. Every stone was turned up to create more business, be it rambling in the Surrey Hills or gliding down to Bournemouth in the Belle. Suburban stations would have enamel notices informing the passenger "to go under the subway for the Surrey Hills".

The three principle constituents, the L.B.S.C.R., S.E. & C.R., and L. & S.W.R., all had glorious histories to add to the Southern; and the Southern could boast, as part of the system, the World's first public railway (the Surrey Iron of 1804) and the first inter-city (Canterbury & Whitstable) built six months before the Liverpool & Manchester. The branch lines of the Southern reflected this history of the original owners, and not one branch line was alike.

In the South East, ancient locomotives and rolling stock contrasted with modern multiple units, and the area became the stamping ground of Colonel Stephens and his activities. On the old "Brighton" system superb Victorian architecture played host to ancient Stroudley engines, whilst in the West every line had a different class of locomotive. Hayling Island used AIXs exclusively until 1963, the Lyme Regis branch used Adams 4-4-2s and Wenford Bridge kept three elderly Beattie well tanks of 1874.

Today many of the branch lines in the country areas have gone for ever, but some have been preserved and preservation is growing. It is still possible to ride behind a 114-year-old engine in Sussex and listen to the distinctive thump of the Westinghouse air pump on the Isle of Wight. Today solid Victorian structures mingle with brand new architecture of the '70s and '80s on modern B.R. The contrast between ancient and modern is truly amazing.

Cowes platform in March 1957 showing parcels being loaded and unloaded into a L.B.S.C.R. coach. Note the board by the nameboard which was used to ramp heavy parcels into the guards brake. At the rear of the station is a noticeboard with handbills tied on with string advertising various excursions on the island.

BRICKLAYERS ARMS

Bricklayers Arms, known to most railway staff as "the Brick", was not so much a branch line as the end of the main line as the South Eastern Railway envisaged it. This short 1¾ mile line was opened to passengers on 1 May 1844 and gave the S.E.R. and the London & Croydon Railway independent access to London without having to pay the swingeing tolls charged by the London & Greenwich Railway over whose tracks the S.E.R. and L. & C. had to ply to get into London Bridge. The South Eastern claimed Bricklayers Arms to be "A Grand West End Terminal" but unfortunately the London & Greenwich reduced the toll so that travel to London Bridge became less expensive. Passengers for the lucrative parts of West End London were none too pleased with being dumped in the Old Kent Road and told to get a cab. Passenger operations ceased by 1852 and thereafter the branch was only used for specials for royalty and other dignitaries until the 1914–1918 war when the line was used for troop transportation. The Southern Railway revived the passenger service for excursions from 1932 until 1939.

In its early days the line was used by several royals including Queen Victoria on her way to Tunbridge Wells in 1849, her eldest daughter, Victoria, on her departure to Germany in 1858, and The Prince of Wales (King Edward VII) in March 1863. Bricklayers Arms is best known for the locomotive depot and the huge goods warehouses and sorting sidings, these all received a great deal of attention during the period 1939–1945 when the branch was bombed by the Luftwaffe on several occasions. Most of the warehouses were gutted and the loco shed damaged. The steam shed was the largest on the S.E.R. and their principle London depot, Bricklayers Arms men had a wide route knowledge and worked to most parts of the system. The loco shed closed in 1962 after the electrification of the South Eastern Division, the last steam locomotive to traverse the branch was probably in 1966 when a Nine Elms "Merchant Navy" was sent round to the workshops for wheel turning.

The branch closed to all traffic on 7 October 1983 with the actual last train running on 6 October 1983. The connection North Kent West to North Kent East closed on 20 June 1981 with the cessation of parcels traffic. The line is at present being sold off for industrial development, the track having been lifted—for enthusiasts of urban and industrial wastage dumping the site is well worth visiting.

DEPTFORD WHARF

This short line from New Cross Gate and Old Kent Road Junction (1865) was opened in 1849 by the London Brighton & South Coast Railway. The line never had a passenger service but was visited on 29 March 1958, and 3 October 1959, by the Railway Correspondence & Travel Society with a special push and pull railmotor set and an H class 0-4-4 tank. The wharf was used for importing coal and timber which was transhipped to barges. The coal went to Waddon Marsh and to the rest of the L.B.S.C.R. system. The branch was worked by L.B.S.C.R. E6 class 0-6-2s in the May 1948 roster, the crews being supplied by Bricklayers Arms men formerly of New Cross Gate. The line closed to freight on 15 October 1963 and little can be seen today as most of the area has been built upon. In an article in July 1973 in the Railway World, W.G. Rugman refers to the Grove Street crossing gates worked from the signal box. The gates had to cover six tracks and must have been one of the longest pairs in existence, so long in fact that it took two men in windy conditions to push them open! Deptford Wharf also had the Grove Street tramway connecting to it and this was worked by the Wharf shunter through the the streets similar to today's Weymouth Quay.

ANGERSTEIN WHARF

This short freight only branch was built privately by Mr. Angerstein who leased it to the S.E.R. The line opened in 1852 and is still in use, the principal traffic being sea dredged ballast landed for Marcon and loaded into 100-ton wagons. The Thames Metal Company also use the line but have not run any scrap trains of late over this short 1-mile branch. The line did have a connection with the L.C.C. tram works which is now owned by Airfix, the works yard abounds with tramway track relics, including conduit-track and tram turntables. Only two known passenger trains have traversed the line—these were two railtours organised by the R.C.T.S. on 29 March 1958 and 3 October 1959.

GREENWICH PARK

The London Chatham & Dover Railway wished to have its own terminus at Greenwich which was opened in 1888. The branch ceased to be of much use after the 1899 amalgamation as it duplicated the more direct South Eastern line. On 1 January 1917 the S.E. & C.R. closed the Greenwich Park branch along with other lines and stations as part of the economies enforced on most railway companies to save manpower, locomotives and rolling stock. Many inner suburban stations were never to reopen but the Greenwich Park branch survived in part. On the completion of the Lewisham loops on 7 July 1929, freight and passenger trains used the former Greenwich Park branch to Nunhead where the line connected with the Catford Loop. An interesting survival of the Greenwich Park branch is the station building at Lewisham Road: although closed in 1917, the station building is complete. Inside can be seen the booking office with ticket office window and waiting rooms. The building is currently in use as a furniture sale room.

CRYSTAL PALACE (HIGH LEVEL)

The L.B. & S.C.R. had already got to Crystal Palace in 1854 with a short branch from the main line at Sydenham. At the close of the Great Exhibition on 11 October 1851, over 6 million people had visited the site in Hyde Park. Public interest was so great that a company was formed to re-erect the building on Sydenham Hill. Leo Schuster, a director of the L.B. & S.C.R., sold his estate of 300 acres to the Crystal Palace Company, and the chairman of the L.B. & S.C.R. became chairman of the Crystal Palace Company. The London Chatham & Dover Railway got in on the act much to the L.B. & S.C.R.'s fury by constructing its own line right up to the front of the Palace, there being an ornate subterranean connection, which still exists, between the site of the Palace and the former High Level station. The High Level branch, opened on 1 August 1865, was a nominally independent company entitled "The Crystal Palace & South London Junction Railway". The railway of course was speculative and ran through a fairly sparsely populated area catching only a few commuters. After the Palace was destroyed by fire in 1936, the potential traffic was even less. The branch was closed temporarily in both wars, from 1 January 1917 to 1 March 1919, and from 22 May 1944 to 4 March 1946. The branch was electrified on 12 July 1925, a substation being built at Upper Sydenham to feed both the High Level branch and the main line in Penge tunnel underneath. Electrification did little to encourage patronage and the line was closed to all traffic by B.R. on 20 September 1954. A special last steam-hauled train was run on Sunday 19 September 1954, hauled by a S.E. & C.R. C class 0-6-0. Enormous crowds turned out to witness the event which was an extremely rare one—the closure of a passenger worked line in the London area. Today most of the line has been built upon but there are relics to be seen, the best being the original station buildings at Upper Sydenham opened in 1884.

ELMERS END TO HAYES AND ADDISCOMBE

The South Eastern Railway country branch line from Elmers End to Hayes still flourishes and, although surrounded by suburbia, the massive overbridges and embankments still suggest the country branch line of 1882. Hayes itself was rebuilt by the Southern just before World War II in 1935, destroyed by bombing in 1940 (they were aiming for Biggin Hill), and rebuilt again by the Southern Region in 1956. Eden Park must be unique for a Southern station in that there is no road to the station—access is by a footpath only. Eden Park is a beautiful survival of a South Eastern Railway country station constructed in Kentish weatherboard. The line, only 3¼ miles long, was opened on 29 May 1882 through rural Kentish countryside, but after electrification in 1925 housing development took off and as a result the line prospered.

Addiscombe was opened in 1864, the same year as Elmers End, and was known as Croydon (Addiscombe Road) until 1 April 1925 when renamed by the Southern Railway. The line was electrified in 1926 and a large carriage depot for multiple unit stock erected. The line today still has a regular interval service and is still signalled by semaphore signals, the box at Addiscombe being of S.E.R. origin. New Beckenham old station, closed in 1864, still survives as a private house known appropriately as "Station House".

WOODSIDE TO SELSDON

This "Croydon avoiding line" was opened on 10 August 1885 from Woodside to Selsdon Road and was jointly owned by the L.B. & S.C.R. and the S.E.R. Opened as the Woodside & South Croydon Railway, the line was worked in alternate years by the two owning companies. The line was closed in 1917 as a wartime economy. The Southern reopened and electrified the line as far as Sanderstead on 30 September 1935. The Southern rebuilt Coombe Road and Bingham Road with the 1935 electrification but had in mind the Southern Heights Railway when electrifying to Selsdon.

The Southern Heights Light Railway was a scheme for an electrified light railway to run from Sanderstead to Orpington with eight intermediate stations. The famous light railway promoter Colonel Stephens had a hand in the scheme but his death in 1931 caused the scheme to fail as the capital had not been raised. The Southern Railway was to work the line which was even shown on Southern carriage maps as a projected railway. The Woodside to Selsdon line closed to all traffic on 16 May 1983 and within a few months was totally demolished—no stations, no track, and partially dismantled bridges. This was one of the quickest branch line demolitions ever carried out. There is a proposal to turn the line into a footpath.

BROMLEY NORTH

The South Eastern Railway got to Bromley after the L.C. & D.R. in 1878 with a short 1½ mile branch from Grove Park which was opened on 1 January 1878. The principle landowner on the line, a Mr. Scott, insisted on a station being sited near his residence, Sundridge Park, for his convenience. The result is the two closest-together stations on B.R., for Sundridge Park is only a ¼-mile from Bromley North—almost a train length. The line was electrified on 28 February 1926, the terminus having been rebuilt by the Southern in 1925. Today the Southern Railway station at Bromley North, recently renovated, stands prominently in the town, a handsome brick building with copper covered cupola.

EPSOM DOWNS

The line from Sutton to Epsom Downs was opened on 22 May 1865 just in time for the races and was double track throughout. Epsom Downs station had nine platforms in its heyday and the monopoly on race traffic until the Tattenham Corner line arrived in 1901. The Epsom Downs line also lost its royal trains to the rival branch. The branch was worked by L.B. & S.C.R. rail motors until electrification on 17 June 1928, although overhead A.C. wiring had been put up on part of the line but was never used. Disaster struck the branch on 16 November 1981 when Epsom Downs signal box was destroyed by fire—the line has been single ever since. An interesting feature of Southern Railway days was the opening of intermediate signal boxes known as A, B, and C; these were only open for the Epsom race week. The semaphore signals carried no spectacles as they were used in daylight hours only. They were abolished in 1955.

CATERHAM & TATTENHAM CORNER

The Caterham branch was opened on 5 August 1856 for both goods and passengers. The railway was an independent company and the S.E.R. or L.B. & S.C.R. were not very interested in purchasing the line, but the S.E.R. eventually bought the line in 1859 after lengthy negotiations. The Centenary of the opening was celebrated on 6 August 1956 with a steam-hauled special hauled by an AIX class 0-6-0; the locomotive was built in 1878, formerly L.B.S.C.R. No 35 "Morden" and numbered DS 377. The engine was painted in Stroudley livery in 1947 and lettered "Loco Works Brighton"—regrettably the engine was broken up in September 1963.

The Tattenham Corner line opened throughout in 1901, the section from Purley to Kingswood & Burgh Heath having been opened on 2 November 1897. The chairman of the S.E. & C.R., Cosmo Bonsor, happened to live at Kingswood and no doubt had some influence over the construction of the line and the grandiose station at Kingswood, itself a delight of late Victorian architecture. Tattenham Corner opened on Derby Day, 4 June 1901, had six platforms, three signal boxes and a special "grandstand" right outside the station. From the prestige point of view, the S.E. & C.R. also stole the royal trains from the "Brighton" and the Queen still travels in a special train to Tattenham Corner even to this day. The regular service to Tattenham Corner lasted until 1907 but was withdrawn until 1928 when the Southern Railway electrified this 8¼ mile long branch. An unusual feature on the line was the tea terrace on the station canopy at Kingswood, possibly unique on a British railway station although common practice in India. The S.E. & C.R. encouraged day trippers to the Chipstead Valley and a tea terrace was provided at Kingswood until World War I. The station buildings at Tattenham Corner are in good repair (where they come under royal scrutiny), which is the exact opposite to the others on the branch which have become tatty and vandalised.

Eden Park on the Hayes branch is a fine example of a South Eastern Railway weatherboard country station of the late nineteenth century. The station is unique to the Southern in that there is no public road access.

Tattenham Corner — the original building of 1901 was built to take large crowds, the race course being right outside the station.

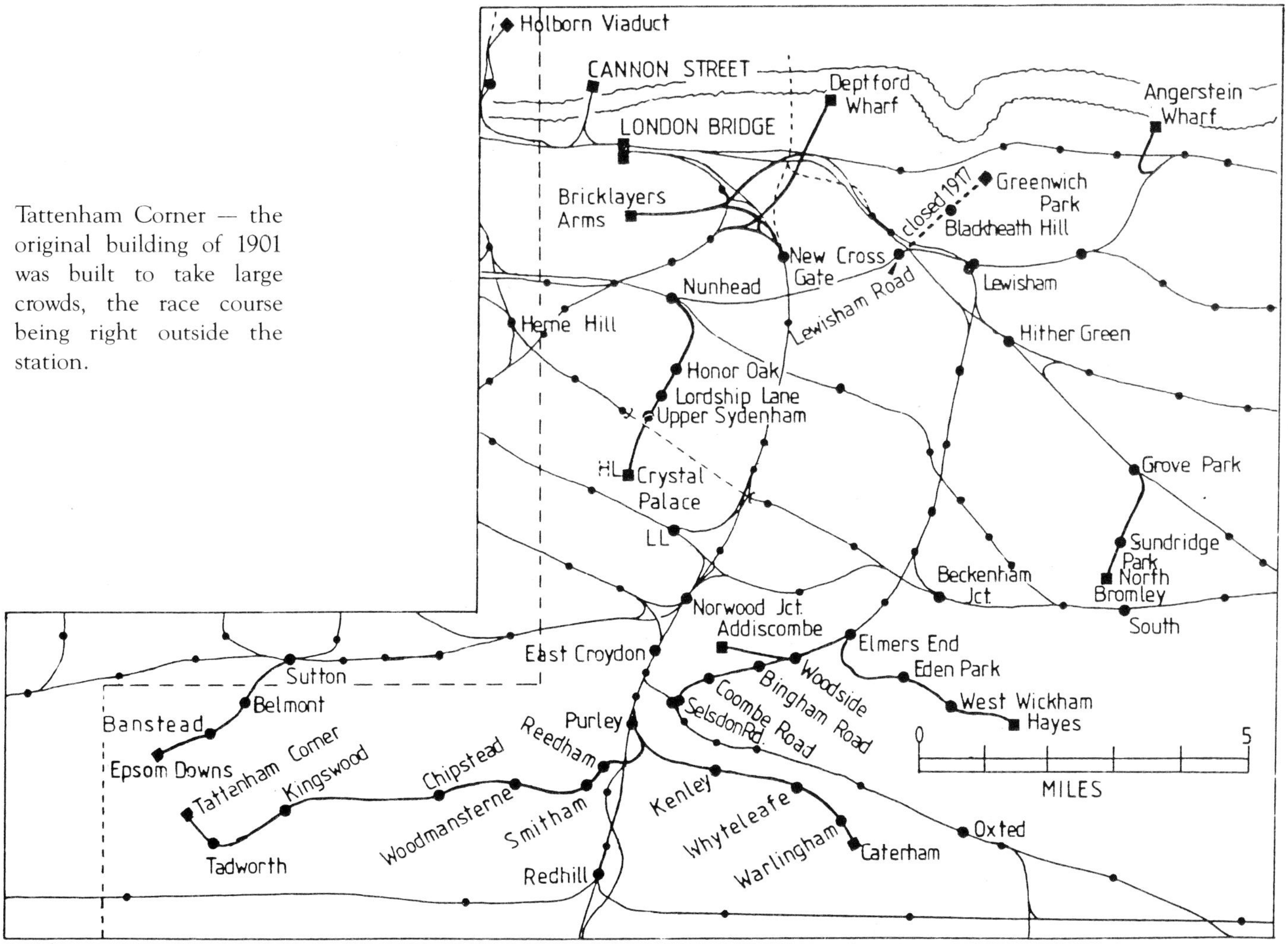

Addiscombe is now the terminus of the Mid Kent line and has a large carriage depot housing EMUT units. The station is still semaphore signalled, unusual for a suburban line, and has a South Eastern Railway box with S.R. and B.R. equipment.

Bromley North has recently been restored and is a fine example of inter-war station architecture of the Southern Railway, having been completely rebuilt by the Southern in 1925 for the electrification of the line.

Engine Workings—London East District (E.R.11)—SATURDAYS 33

BRICKLAYERS ARMS DUTY No. 100

3 P. (E.1 Class.)

Off **Friday**

C—Shunting 12.0 mdt. to 1.15 a.m.

Arr.	Station	Dep.	
—	Cannon Street	1.34 a.m.	**E**
1.54 a.m.	Rotherhithe Road ...	2. 0 a.m.	H
2.10 a.m.	Bricklayers Arms Loco.	5. 0 a.m.	‖
••	Rotherhithe Road ...	5.30 a.m.	**E**
6. 6 a.m.	Holborn (**S.R.E.**)... ...	6.56 a.m.	**E**
	(via Orpington)		
7.12 a.m.	London Bridge	7.24 a.m.	**P**
8.50 a.m.	Ashford...	8.56 a.m.	**P**
10.30 a.m.	Ramsgate	••	‖
••	Loco. Yard	8.50 p.m.	‖
••	Ramsgate	9.10 p.m.	**P**
	(via Blackheath)		
12.29 a.m.	Charing Cross	••	‖
••	Cannon Street	—	
	C—Shunting 1.45 a.m. to 2.0 a.m.		
—	Cannon Street	2. 0 a.m.	**E**
	(after 9.28 p.m. Margate)		
2.25 a.m.	Rotherhithe Road ...	••	‖
••	Bricklayers Arms Loco.	—	

Bricklayers Arms Men.

1st set on duty 4.0 a.m., relieved at London Bridge at 7.13 a.m., passenger to Bricklayers Arms, relieve No. 135 at 8.37 a.m., work and dispose.

2nd set on duty 6.45 a.m., relieve at London Bridge 7.20 a.m., relieved at Ashford at 8.50 a.m., as ordered, relieve No. 432 at 11.50 a.m., work and relieved in depot.

Ramsgate Men.

Off No. 488, relieve at Ashford at 8.50 a.m., work and commence disposal.

Off No. 471, finish disposal.

Off No. 494, prepare for 8.50 p.m. ‖.

Faversham Men.

1st set on duty 6.40 p.m., passenger per 7.5 p.m. to Ramsgate Depot, relieve at 8.50 p.m. ‖, relieved Chatham at 10.55 p.m., relieve No. 172 at Chatham Sidings at 11.37 p.m., work and dispose.

[*continued*

BRICKLAYERS ARMS DUTY No. 100—*continued.*

Gillingham Men.

1st set on duty 10.25 p.m., passenger per 10.50 p.m., and relieve same at Chatham at 10.55 p.m., work and relieved in depot, prepare No. 123 (**Sunday**) for 3.50 a.m. ‖, work and change with No. 60 (**Sunday**) at Strood at 5.44 a.m., work and relieved at Gillingham at 6.30 a.m.

Bricklayers Arms Men.

Sunday—P. and D. men dispose.

No. 101—NOT USED.

Deptford Wharf North box was the original when this photograph was taken in 1958 on the occasion of an R.C.T.S. railtour. The signalbox had some of the original instruments from the opening of the line, one of the repeaters being marked "L.B.S.C.R. 1849". Note the bell on the roof and the double folding gates which had to cross six tracks and were two-man operated. The railtour engine is an H class 0-4-4 tank, whilst the regular freight is hauled by an E6 class 0-6-2 tank. The yard is now a housing estate and the only thing left today is the factory chimney.

Bricklayers Arms apart from the freight depots also housed the principal engine shed for the area. A copy of Duty 100, one of the most popular turns from the shed, is shown. Bricklayers Arms men had a wide route knowledge on Central and South Eastern Divisions. The E1 or D1 class would work right through to Ramsgate and back by both routes—this was a popular turn with railway enthusiasts who would crowd on to the first coach of the 7.24 a.m. London Bridge for a fast run down the main line. This train ran until 1961.

Kingswood & Burgh Heath Station was unique. The S.E. & C.R. opened the line from Purley in 1897 and the stations were individually designed. The railway company wanted to encourage day trippers into the countryside and a facility was provided for them. A tea terrace was built over the platform canopy as illustrated and was in use until World War I. This facility is common enough in the Indian sub continent, where no doubt the architect gained his ideas, but unique to a British railway station.

Epsom Dow
has now bee
reduced to t
platforms—
originally th
grand termi
had nine
platforms,
water tank,
coal stage,
turntable an
extensive
sidings.

Hayes station was bombed during World War II when the Luftwaffe dropped a few kilos on the way to nearby Biggin Hill. The station was rebuilt after the war and still serves the community well. The upper picture shows Hayes today and the lower in S.E. & C.R. days. Note that the only feature to survive are the buffer-stops, still intact today!

Coombe Road was one of the Southern's recent closures, being closed completely on 16 May 1983 and demolished shortly afterwards. There is a proposal to turn the line from Woodside to Selsdon into a footpath. Picture above shows the station in 1983, and below a few months later—now you see it, now you don't!

Upper Sydenham Station after closure of the Crystal Palace High Level branch which closed in September 1954. The station house is still in use as a private dwelling and the trackbed is now a park. Photograph taken four years after closure in 1958.

Upper Sydenham in B.R. days prior to closure in 1954 with 4 SUB unit No 4671. The branch had a chequered history and was closed in both wars. Electrification took place in 1925 and the service was to Blackfriars from Crystal Palace High Level.

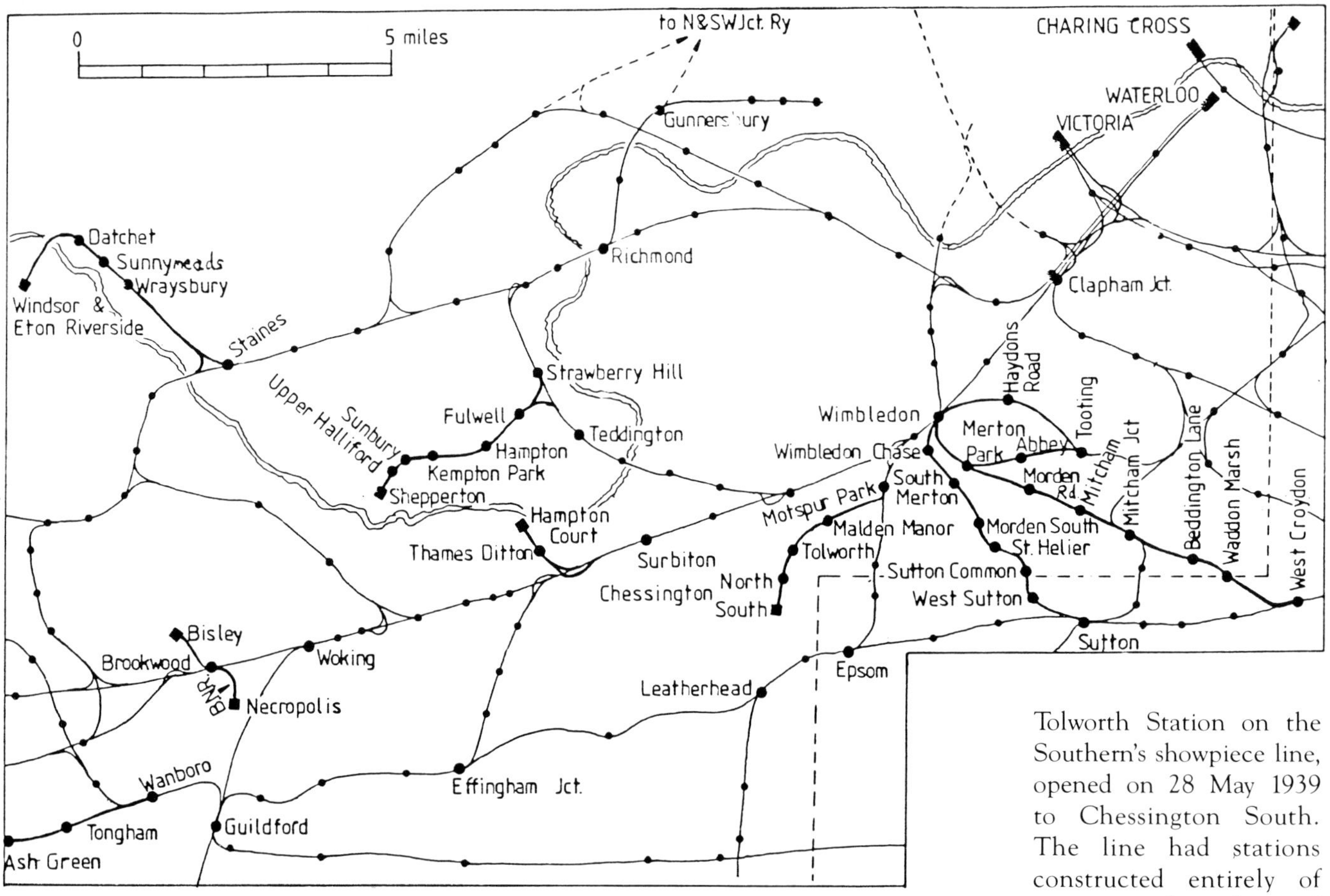

Tolworth Station on the Southern's showpiece line, opened on 28 May 1939 to Chessington South. The line had stations constructed entirely of concrete and was designed to take large crowds at peak periods.

WEST CROYDON TO WIMBLEDON

A cross-country line mostly single track which, before being engulfed by London suburbia, could have been termed "a branch line". Even today the line has a rural appearance about it not associated with suburban lines. The line was opened on 22 October 1855 and electrified on 6 July 1930, the multiple unit trains displaced the push & pull service inaugurated by the L.B.S.C.R. in 1919. Electrification has probably saved the line from closure, the 2 SUB units that were introduced were conversions from the South London line stock of 1909. These units had a long internal side corridor, a feature of L.B.S.C.R. rolling stock. The West Croydon to Wimbledon line is built partially over the course of the Surrey Iron Railway of 1804—the world's first public railway. One or two features of this historic line can still be seen. The station building at Mitcham, formally a private house, has "Tramway Path" alongside it, as also does the Surrey Iron Hackbridge branch. The Hackbridge branch of the Surrey Iron can still be discerned alongside the main road from Mitcham Common to Hackbridge. This must have been the first branch line on a public railway; the Surrey Iron was horse-worked and regarded as a public right of way very much like a modern road.

MERTON ABBEY

Prior to electrification of the Tooting to Wimbledon lines in 1929, the service to Wimbledon was on a loop line via Merton Abbey or Haydons Road. The line was known by railway staff as the Wimbledon "pear". With electrification, the Merton Abbey section was closed on 3 March 1929, the line having been closed from 1917 to 1923 anyway. The opening of the Northern Line of London Transport in 1926 did a lot to kill off the passenger traffic potential on the line. The Merton Abbey branch did stay open to freight until 5 May 1975, having been opened jointly by the L.B. & S.C. and the L.S.W.R. on 1 October 1868. Today little remains to be seen as the station at Merton Abbey has been engulfed by a scrapyard, although "Station Road" still exists. There is a proposal to turn Merton Park to Tooting into a public footpath to be known locally as "Mugger's Paradise".

THE WIMBLEDON & SUTTON RAILWAY

This suburban link from the former L.S.W.R. main line at Wimbledon to Sutton was opened for traffic on 5 January 1930 and was electrified from the outset. The line could hardly be termed a branch line but had many features common to the forthcoming Chessington branch of 1939. The Wimbledon & Sutton was built to keep the District railway out of Sutton and more importantly the City & South London, Morden extension away from Southern territory. Today the Northern Line terminates almost head on with the Wimbledon & Sutton near Morden South. The large housing estates of the twenties justified the construction of the line which has island platform stations and horrific gradients. The steepest part being the 1 in 44 between West Sutton and Sutton over which steam locomotives were banned.

THE CHESSINGTON SOUTH BRANCH

The railway opened throughout on 28 May 1939 and was one of the Southern's showpieces. The stations were built in concrete and had awnings entitled "Chisarc cantilevered reinforced concrete", similar to L.T. stations in the outer suburbs. This 4¼ mile long line is certainly thriving and, peering over the fences of some of the intermediate stations, the passenger has the impression of endless suburbia spreading for miles and miles over the horizon. The line was intended to go through to Leatherhead but the 1939–1945 war knocked that on the head and the line today terminates at Chessington South, designed to be an intermediate station. The branch terminates so abruptly that within a few minutes' walk the passenger finds himself in open country with suburbia behind him. Passengers arriving at Chessington South are reminded by a B.R. notice which refers to "Zoo Pedestrians"—presumably for animals that can read, as well as humans!

HAMPTON COURT

The short branch from Hampton Court Junction on the main line of only 2 miles crosses the four-track main line on the handsome brick-built viaduct of 1915. The Hampton Court line was included in the first round of L.S.W.R. electrification (1915–1916). The line was electrified on 18 June 1916 on 660 volt D.C. current with conductor rail. Hampton Court station in Victorian gothic was opened on 1 February 1849 and presents a rather tatty appearance to visitors today.

SHEPPERTON

This line was mooted as the "Thames Valley Railway" and opened on 1 November 1864, the L.S.W.R. taking over in 1865. The line was one of the first to be electrified by the L.S.W.R., being opened for electric traction on 30 January 1916. The L.S.W.R. had adopted the third rail D.C. scheme following a visit by officials to study the New York system. The Americans must have done a good selling job to the L.S.W.R. resulting in the system being adopted as standard for the whole of the Southern. A pity that the L.S.W.R. did not adopt an overhead electrification system, as every railwayman and commuter can testify to this day. One unusual feature of the Shepperton branch is the station at Kempton Park which has no public access, not even a footpath! The station is used for the races and was opened in 1878 although the present structure probably dates from the 1890 rebuild.

WINDSOR & ETON RIVERSIDE

Windsor & Eton was opened on 1 December 1849, being 6¾ miles from Staines and having a fine gothic terminal building of an individual design, the architect being Sir William Tite. The line was electrified on 6 July 1930. The section of Waterloo station where Windsor and Reading trains terminate is known as the "Windsor lines" as is also the four tracks from Waterloo to Clapham Junction. This would infer that the line from Waterloo goes to Windsor and that Windsor could not be termed a branch line in the true sense.

BISLEY

This short branch was opened from Brookwood on 12 July 1890 to Bisley Camp for the National Rifle Assoc., the N.R.A. having been transferred from Wimbledon Common. The branch was not advertised in the public timetable, but was shown on Southern Railway maps and was closed to all traffic on 21 July 1952. The line was rail-toured with a push & pull unit after closure.

BROOKWOOD NECROPOLIS

The Brookwood Cemetery branch was opened in 1854 and through trains were run from a special station alongside the L.S.W.R. at Waterloo. The Waterloo terminus alongside Waterloo main station had two platforms and the entrance was in Westminster Bridge Road. From here the L.S.W.R. ran through trains for the Necropolis Company to the cemetery which had two stations. Trains ran until 1941 but in May of that year the train and station at Waterloo were destroyed by bombing. The stations at the cemetery were intact until recently, but the south station was destroyed by fire in September 1972, the North having already been demolished. A curious feature was that each corpse was issued with a ticket for the journey from Waterloo—no returns, only singles! Part of the line today is a public footpath.

H class 0-4-4 No 31521 with a railtour in 1958 at Merton Abbey, closed to passengers in 1929. This site is now a scrapyar but the over bridge still exists.

Windsor & Eton sees a rare event in 1957 with a steam hauled excursion hauled by "Remembrance" class 4-6-0 No 32331 "Beattie" on a scout special for London Bridge. The "Remembrance" class was a rare class of 4-6-0 of which there were only seven examples—they were Maunsell rebuilds of the L.B. & S.C.R. L class 4-6-4T of 1914. They were classified N15X and disappeared in the 1950s.

Hampton Court was one of the earliest L. & S.W.R. branch lines, having been opened in 1849. The station's architect is assumed to be Sir William Tite, the same architect as for Windsor & Eton.

Brookwood, with the "Bisley Bullet" in Southern Railway days, with D1 class 0-4-2T No 2260 and L. & S.W.R. push & pull set. The Bisley branch was unusual in that the trains were not shown in the timetable. The line closed to all traffic on 21 July 1952.

Shepperton, the end of the L. & S.W.R. branch from Strawberry Hill, was opened in 1864 and rather tatty in 1986.

GRAVESEND WEST

This 4½ mile long branch was opened as late as 17 April 1886, the rival South Eastern Railway having got to Gravesend in 1849 by the North Kent Railway. There were three intermediate stations on the line, Longfield, Southfleet, and Rosherville, built to serve the nearby Rosherville Gardens, a resort for day trippers. Rosherville closed on 15 July 1933 having been reduced to a halt status. A feature of the line was that boat trains ran from 1916 to 1940 to connect with a boat to Holland; the train started from Victoria, included a Pullman and was usually short enough to be hauled by an H class 0-4-4 tank. The line closed to passenger traffic on 3 August 1953. Freight traffic over the line lasted until 29 March 1968 from Southfleet to Gravesend, the section from Southfleet closing on 26 January 1976 to Fawkham Junction. Proposals have recently been mooted for a steam-worked preservation line but so far nothing has come of it. The track has been removed between Gravesend and Southfleet. The section from Fawkham Junction to Gravesend may be turned into a public footpath in the future.

WESTERHAM

This was another rural South Eastern Railway branch which nearly made it to the preservation scene. Had the line been preserved, it would have been a great success as it was near to London and could take the largest locomotives—even Bulleid 4-6-2s. The line was opened amid much ceremony on 6 July 1881, and was one of the first to have steam railmotors introduced to the line in April 1906. Push & Pull working with S.E. & C.R. standard P or H classes followed and this was the method of line working right up to complete closure which was from 30 October 1961. The closure of the line was hastened by political interests as the present M25 motorway runs over most of the site of the line. A preservation society was formed, the Westerham Valley Railway Association, but little co-operation was offered by the authorities as the Sevenoaks bypass and M25 needed the railway land. There was however some small benefit in that an H class 0-4-4 and C class 0-6-0 were bought for the line and can now be seen running on the Bluebell Railway, Sussex. These two locomotives have been restored to their S.E. & C.R. brunswick green and are numbered 263 and 1592 respectively. The branch to Westerham was always popular with visiting enthusiasts and was within easy reach of London.

PADDOCK WOOD TO HAWKHURST

The Hawkhurst branch could be described as everybody's favourite. The line was steam worked, single track, passed through picturesque countryside and ran from nowhere to nowhere. The single track line left the main line at Paddock Wood and headed off southwards across the Kentish hopfields. There were three intermediate stations at Horsmonden, Goudhurst and Cranbrook on the 11½ mile journey to Hawkhurst. The South Eastern Railway promoted the line and opened it on 4 September 1893 for they were determined to keep the L.C. & D.R. out of their territory. The railway was engineered by the then youthful Holman F. Stephens who was appointed at the age of 22 as resident engineer. Later as Colonel Stephens, he was to manage and build a large number of light railways throughout the country.

Hawkhurst was originally planned for electrification on the stage 2 Kent electrification schemes of the 1960s, but owing to financial cutbacks something had to go. It would be interesting to see what the line would be like today had it been electrified. A curious feature of the line in steam days were the hop-pickers specials from London Bridge, usually worked by an ancient S.E. & C.R. locomotive and true to form running via very devious routes to get to the branch. Mechanisation of hop picking did away with this unusual traffic shortly before the line closed to all traffic on 12 June 1961. Today, Horsmonden station can still be seen in use as a local garage, as also can Cranbrook, now a private house and formerly a pottery. Hawkhurst station has been demolished but the signal box still survives, having been restored and repainted.

ALLHALLOWS & GRAIN

The South Eastern Railway opened up Port Victoria station and pier on 11 September 1882 from Hoo Junction on the Isle of Grain. The rival L.C.D.R. had opened a pier on the opposite side of the Medway at Queenborough Pier on 15 May 1876. Port Victoria was used by boat trains until May 1904, thereafter only local branch trains to Gravesend used the line which was used by royalty and was popular with Queen Victoria as few people were there to see the trains. The Port Victoria ordinary passenger services were discontinued on 11 June 1951, the pier having slipped quietly into the Medway. From 4 September 1951 a new station was opened at Grain which was for workers at the nearby oil refinery of vast acreage. Passenger services to Grain and Allhallows ceased on 4 December 1961, The oil network at Grain now obliterates all signs of the former S.E.R. Port Victoria line and oil tank trains still run to Grain from Hoo Junction although the BP refinery ceased operating in 1983. A strange twist in the fortunes of the branch being that now North Sea oil is used, there is no need to import Middle East oil at this location.

The Grain branch was connected by a new line from Stoke Junction to Allhallows opened by the Southern Railway on 16 May 1932. This 1¾ mile long line was promoted by the Southern with the intention of capturing the commuter and day tripper traffic to the new speculative beach resort of Allhallows-on-Sea. The intended property development did not take place and the line was closed to all traffic on 4 December 1961. Now, 25 years later, guess what's happened? Property development has increased, holiday caravan parks have been built, new estates, shops and schools have been constructed—the whole place is booming! The perfect irony is the caravan park, Kingsmead Park, built on the site of the station—only the water tower survives to remind residents that this was once the station. The Southern Railway were right but they opened the Allhallows line 30 years too soon!

THE SHEPPEY LIGHT (LEYSDOWN–QUEENBOROUGH)

This standard gauge branch of 8¾ miles ran eastwards from Queenborough on the Sheerness line and was constructed as a light railway under the 1896 act, the engineer being H.F. Stephens. The line opened for traffic on 1 August 1901 and became part of the S.E. & C.R. network. The intermediate stations had the Colonel Stephens look about them—with the use of corrugated iron and timber materials, the structures were cheaper than brick or stone. Today, no doubt, plastics would have been used had such building materials been available at the time. The S.E. & C.R. bought a L.B. & S.C. AIX class No 654 for use on the line in 1905 and this was numbered into S.E. & C.R. stock as No 751. This locomotive is now in Montreal at the Canadian Railroad Museum. The S.E. & C.R. tried steam railmotors but they had limited fuel and water capacity, so conventional S.E.R. or L.C.D.R. locomotives were used until closure on 4 December 1950 to all traffic. At closure the articulated push & pull railmotor sets were still in use—these were conversions from the S.E. & C.R. steam railcars of 1905 and lasted well into B.R. days. The articulated sets could be seen at work on the Westerham branch well into the 1950s. Little evidence of the Leysdown branch can be seen today as the line had fairly light engineering works and a great deal of the old track bed has been lost to view by being ploughed up by farmers.

SHEERNESS & QUEENBOROUGH PIER

The Sheerness branch opened on 19 July 1860 from Sittingbourne and the connection facing London giving direct running to Sheerness from the London direction came into use in 1863–64. Regular passenger services could be withdrawn over the direct line to the Sheerness branch in 1986. Access to Sheerness on the Isle of Sheppey was over the Swale at Kingsferry bridge which had a lifting section to allow ships to pass. This bridge was so decrepit that it was always jamming causing considerable disruption to South Eastern Division services during the years prior to electrification in 1959. The Kingsferry bridge was rebuilt and now carries road and rail together. The L.C. & D.R. built a short branch to Queenborough Pier which was opened on 15 May 1876, a boat train service was provided which connected with the Zeeland Steamship Company's service to Flushing in Holland. The Pier closed to all traffic on 1 March 1923; Sheerness Dockyard closed just before grouping on 2 January 1922.

THE CANTERBURY & WHITSTABLE RAILWAY

The first railway in Kent and one of the first public railways between two towns to be built using steam traction—the line from Canterbury West to Whitstable even preceded the Liverpool & Manchester and was opened in May 1830. The Liverpool & Manchester was opened in September 1830, six months later. The line engineered by the Stephensons was mostly cable worked with one level section worked by a steam locomotive "Invicta", an 0-4-0, which was the twenty-fourth engine to be built by Stephenson. The locomotive is preserved in the National Collection but at present is not on view to the public. The Canterbury & Whitstable line was bought by the South Eastern Railway in 1853, passenger services ceased on 31 December 1930 and freight on 1 December 1952. The line had restricted clearances through Tyler Hill tunnel which meant that the locomotives using the branch had to have cut down boiler mountings. One of the little known features of the line was the bridge over the public road at Whitstable, by Whitstable & Tankerton station, which had a plaque attached to the abutment claiming it to be the first bridge by rail over road. The bridge has since been demolished and the road widened.

RAMSGATE HARBOUR & MARGATE SANDS

The two old rivals, the L.C. & D.R. and the S.E.R., had duplicated the railway network in the Margate and Ramsgate area. The L.C. & D.R. had a "main line" to Ramsgate Harbour (the building still exists) which was on the beach and reached over a steep gradient through a tunnel. The S.E.R. main line ran to Ramsgate Town but had a branch to Margate—all trains for Margate had to reverse in Ramsgate Town station. With effect from 2 July 1926, the layout was simplified and trains now run round the coast on a loop between Margate, Broadstairs, and Ramsgate.

FOLKESTONE HARBOUR

This is a short ¾ mile long line from Folkestone Junction down to Folkestone Harbour on an average gradient of 1 in 30—one of the steepest lines on the present B.R. system. The South Eastern Railway opened the line in 1849 having bought the Harbour in 1843. The railway to Folkestone Harbour was one of the causes of Dover people backing the direct line from Dover to London, which later became the London, Chatham & Dover Railway, the South Eastern's cursed rival. Folkestone Harbour to Folkestone Junction was one of the most spectacular lines on B.R. for steam trains as they were worked by four locomotives, sometimes two at the front and two at the back but quite frequently by triple headers with one engine on the rear. Triple heading was extremely rare on a British railway—a sight not easily forgotten. The trains were worked by S.E.R. 0-6-0 RI class tanks which in 1959 were superseded by G.W.R. panniers. The line was electrified in 1961.

THE EAST KENT LIGHT RAILWAY (SHEPHERDSWELL–WINGHAM)

This was one of the Colonel Stephens lines in Kent, the first step in construction was to Tilmanstone Colliery just over a mile from Shepherdswell on the main L.C.D.R. Faversham to Dover line. Coal in Kent had been discovered when boring for the Channel Tunnel, and Shepherdswell to Tilmanstone Colliery was opened on 27 November 1912. The passenger service to Wingham on the E.K.R. was inaugurated on 16 October 1916. An extension from Eastry on the Wingham line opened to Richborough Port on the coast near Pegwell Bay in December 1916. The Richborough line was to a wartime harbour including train ferries and extensive marshalling yards. The loading of the ships continued until the end of 1918 with wartime armaments and stores, but an ordinary passenger service was not opened up until 1925 and only then to Sandwich Road. The East Kent built a station at Richborough but it was never used—in fact it never had any track. The Wingham line was extended to Canterbury Road in 1925—a remote spot in the middle of nowhere, in fact 6 miles from Canterbury! The Eastry to Sandwich Road branch closed on 1 November 1928 to passengers. Extensions were planned to the system and work was carried out on branches to Deal, Birchington and Canterbury but, with the death of Colonel Stephens in 1931, work ceased on further extensions to the system which were based on the premise that more collieries would be opened. The Richborough Port section saw service again during World War II but was closed completely on 27 October 1949. The line from Canterbury Road closed to passengers on 1 November 1948; B.R., the new owners, had not wasted much time in cutting out this uneconomic branch. By 1 July 1951 there was no freight beyond Tilmanstone, which was still open to the colliery in 1984. The future of the Kentish Coalfield looks bleak—Tilmanstone and Betteshanger are on the N.C.B. list of closures for the 1980s and Snowdown has already closed. Tilmanstone has had no trains since the 1984 coal strike and may never reopen. The line is 2 miles 69 chains long.

The East Kent had a hotch-potch of secondhand locomotives and rolling stock mainly purchased from the neighbouring Southern. An interesting survival is L.S.W.R. 4-4-2 No 488, built in 1882 by Neilson & Co., which was acquired by the Bluebell Railway in 1961 and can still be seen at work today.

THE KENT & EAST SUSSEX RAILWAY (HEADCORN TO ROBERTSBRIDGE)

This was probably the most successful of the Colonel Stephens group of railways and like the East Kent was nationalised on 1 January 1948. The K. & E.S.R. is also partly in use today, a regular service being run for most of the year from Tenterden using vintage locomotives and rolling stock. There is a museum at Tenterden about Colonel Stephens and his activities, including many personal relics. The line was opened in 1900 as the Rother Valley Railway from Robertsbridge to Rolvenden (then called Tenterden) and extended to Headcorn in 1904 as the K.E.S.R. The railway lasted into B.R. days and was not closed to passengers until 4 January 1954. The section from Headcorn to Tenterden was closed to all traffic on that date and the remainder from Tenterden to Robertsbridge on 12 June 1961 to freight.

In 1961 the Kent & East Sussex Railway Association was formed and after lengthy negotiations, court cases, and a change of government, the line eventually received its Light Railway Transfer Order and reopened as the Tenterden Railway Company on 3 February 1974. This says much for the tenacity and determination of railway preservationists and the hope for the future is to extend the line to Bodiam where there is a fine moated castle a short walk from the station. The present line runs from Tenterden to Wittersham Road, a spot in the middle of nowhere. The present K. & E.S.R. has a varied collection of locomotives and rolling stock including two AIX class 0-6-0s, one of which was an original K. & E.S.R. engine, being ex-L.B. & S.C.R. No 70 "Poplar" of 1872 vintage. This engine is still working and must be one of the world's oldest regularly working locomotives, being 114 years old. Colonel Stephens would have been proud of the present set-up, had he been able to see it today!

NEW ROMNEY & DUNGENESS

The line from Appledore on the Ashford to Hastings line was opened on 7 December 1881 to Dungeness for freight and 1 April 1883 for passengers. The New Romney branch opened on 19 June 1884 for all traffic, and both Dungeness and New Romney became part of the South Eastern Railway system, the Lydd Railway Company having been absorbed in 1895. The South Eastern Railway were proposing to open a port at Dungeness and run a steamer service to France. The New Romney and Dungeness branches were certainly unusual as they ran from Lydd Town across miles and miles of shingle—a relic of the sea having receded over several centuries. New Romney and Rye were at one time on the coast. The Southern Railway realigned the New Romney line in June 1937 and brought the whole line nearer to the coastal stretch, they also opened new stations at Lydd and Greatstone-on-Sea, hoping to tap the traffic from the coastal holiday camps which sprang up in the 1920s to 1930s. The Romney Hythe and Dymchurch Railway had been opened along the coast from Dungeness to New Romney in 1929—this 15-inch gauge line of course still runs in the summer. New Romney survived into the diesel age and eventually closed to all traffic from New Romney to Lydd on-Sea on 6 March 1967 and passengers to Appledore. Today the Power Station at Dungeness still has use for the line with container traffic. An unusual event of recent years was a Branch Line Society Special with a 6L DEMU set from Appledore to Dungeness on Saturday, 19 January 1985. The fare for the two trips to the Power Station siding was a mere £6.95 return for the 9½ mile journey. This certainly was a coup for the Society as the Southern Region are reluctant to allow passenger trains over goods-only lines nowadays.

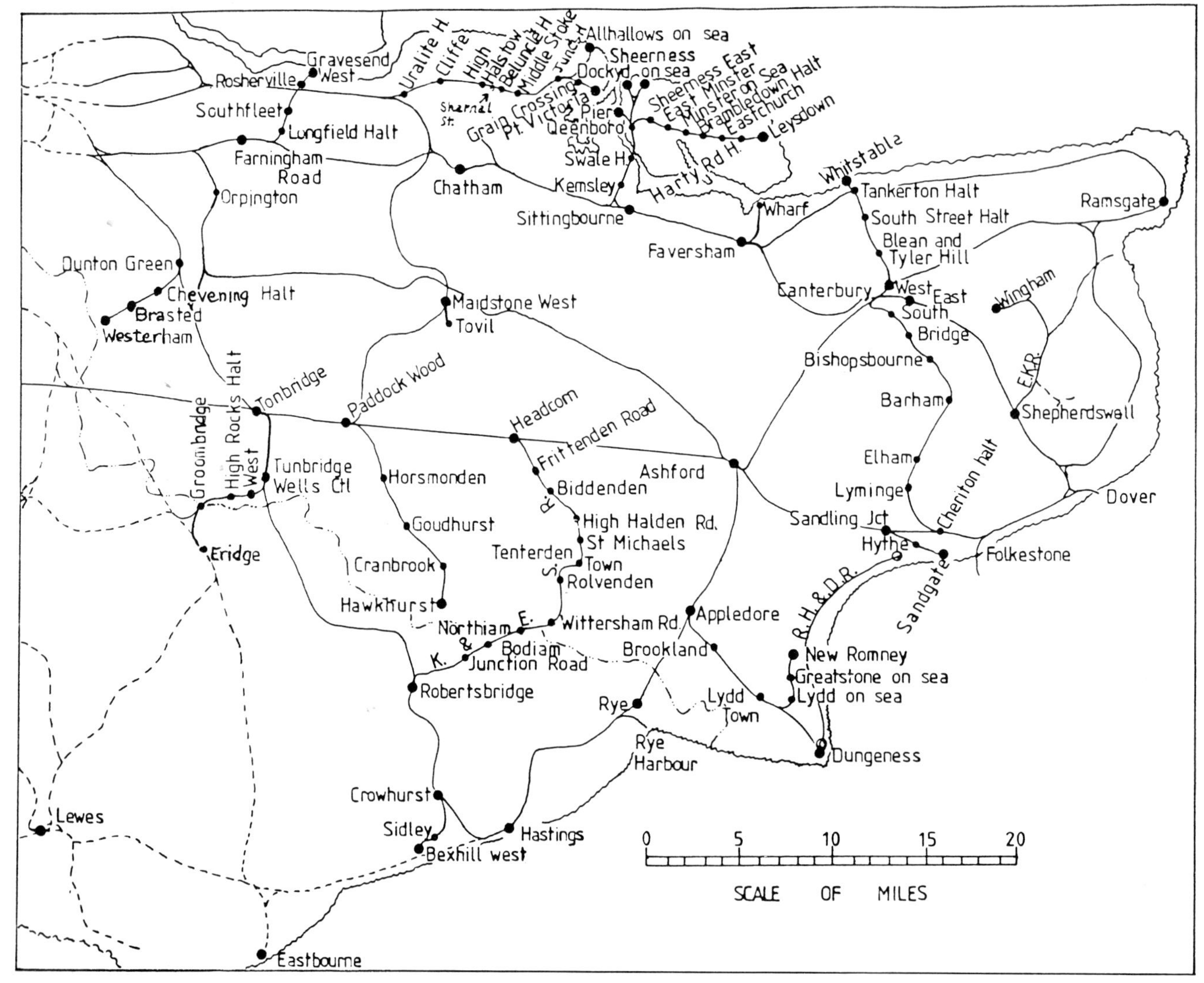

THE ELHAM VALLEY RAILWAY (CANTERBURY WEST–SHORNCLIFFE)

The branch line from Canterbury to Folkestone, Harbledown Junction to Cheriton Junction to be precise, was 16¼ miles in length and traversed picturesque unspoilt Kentish countryside. The line was built mainly to keep the rival London Chatham & Dover Railway away from the South Eastern's territory and was opened on 1 July 1889. The line had a chequered career. During World War II the Elham Valley was taken over by the army and a rail mounted gun trundled up and down the line, occasionally firing off shells from its mounted 16-inch naval gun. The Luftwaffe were always trying to find the gun which was used to shell France, and several incidents occurred with the line being bombed or shot up. The Imperial War Museum have a photograph of the Prime Minister inspecting the gun at Bishopsbourne in 1941. The Southern Railway closed the line to all traffic from 16 June 1947. Two of the stations survive today, having been converted to private houses. Bishopsbourne, the third station down the branch from Canterbury, was the station where Eustace Missenden, a future General Manager of the Southern Railway, started work as a ticket clerk in 1899.

HYTHE & SANDGATE

This short branch was opened on 9 October 1874 from Sandling Junction to Sandgate, the intermediate station being at Hythe. The South Eastern Railway ran a connecting tramway, horse worked, from Sandgate to Hythe, Hythe S.E.R. station being somewhat inconveniently situated to the town. Sandgate closed on 1 April 1931, and the piece from Hythe to Sandling Junction on 3 December 1951.

MISCELLANEOUS LINES

The London, Chatham & Dover Railway opened a short branch to Faversham Creek in April 1860 for goods traffic. This was closed during B.R. days. The L.C. & D.R. also had a branch to Ashford (the Maidstone & Ashford Railway); this terminated at Ashford L.C. & D.R. station, a four platform terminal. Upon amalgamation, the S.E. & C.R. closed Ashford L.C. & D.R. and the old terminus to passengers, the trains being diverted to Ashford main line station. Thus Maidstone and Ashford is no longer a branch line but a through route used by boat trains, especially in the busy summer months. A similar situation existed at Sevenoaks where the now through route from Sevenoaks via Otford was a L.C. & D.R. branch from Swanley Junction. The present Ashford to Ore line is now reduced to single line status from Appledore and this once main line could almost be termed a branch. Tovil Goods in Maidstone closed to all traffic on 3 October 1977.

Westerham Station with ex- L.B. & S.C.R. set No 723 in B.R. red livery. Note the Southern station nameboard in white on green enamel and the old rails used in the construction.

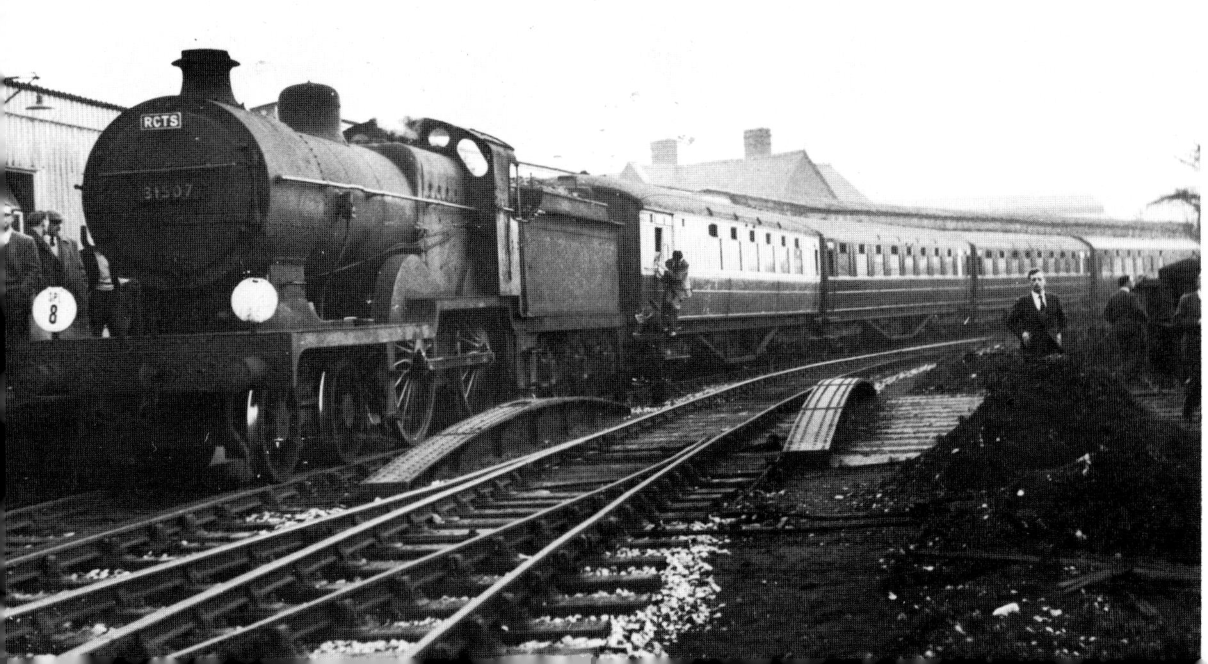

Gravesend West with a special train and an E1 class 4-4-0 in March 1959. The special started at Liverpool Street, went via Snow Hill and consisted of Gresley stock only.

The Westerham push and pull nears Brasted shortly before closure in 1961. The site is now part of the M25 motorway.

The scene in the 1970s, with the station awaiting demolition for the M25 motorway.

Scenes on the Grain branch with H class 0-4-4T No 31517 and passenger train waiting at the Grain passenger terminal opened to serve the nearby oil refinery in the upper picture and Middle Stoke Halt in the lower. The Halt at Middle Stoke was of the standard Southern Railway all-concrete design. The line closed to passengers on 4 December 1961, though at present oil trains still run to Grain.

Sharnall Street, with S.E. & C.R. 0-4-4T No 1308 resplendent in Southern livery, and L.B. & S.C.R. stock. The branch is still in use, as oil trains still run to Grain refinery, but the picturesque country station at Sharnall Street has been demolished.

Allhallows-on-Sea with the last train on 3 December 1961 with C class 0-6-0 No 31689. Allhallows was not opened until May 1932 by the Southern Railway to develop the seaside resort—ironically the site is now a mobile homes colony. The water tower still survives today.

Queenborough, formerly the junction for the Sheppey Light Railway, sees Ivatt class 2 2-6-2T arriving with a Sheerness to Sittingbourne train. The conductor rails have been laid for the 1959 Kent Coast electrification. The Leysdown line started in a bay platform behind the waiting shelter on the right.

The Sheppey Light was worked by an A1 0-6-0T purchased from the L.B. & S.C.R. in 1905, formerly No 54 "Waddon"—the loco ended its working life at Lancing works in 1963. The engine is now fully restored and can be seen at the Canadian Railroad Museum at Montreal.

On the Elham Valley Railway, Bridge Station has been turned into a private house.

Bishopsbourne as seen from th road overbridge in the pre-w period when the line was single Bishopsbourne is still there tod just as seen in the photograp although the track was remove after closure in June 1947.

Hythe, the terminus of the short branch from Sandling Junction, with R1 class No 31671 (ex-L.C. & D.R.) and railmotor for Ashford. The line closed to all traffic on 31 December 1951.

The Canterbury & Whitstable Railway was an early inter-city railway and can claim to be older than the Liverpool & Manchester by six months. The line was engineered by the Stephensons, father and son, but was steeply graded. Locomotives had to have cut down boiler mountings for the very narrow tunnel clearances. In the top picture an R1 class 0-6-0 No 31010 tackles the grade out of Canterbury. The centre picture shows the World's first railway bridge over a road—a plaque on the wall was erected by the Whitstable Historical Society. The bridge has since been demolished and the road widened. The lower picture shows South Street Halt with the Rochester Way roadbridge in the background. The road bridge is still there and the trackbed is now a footpath through a housing estate. The line closed to passengers from 1 January 1931 and freight on 1 December 1952.

A rare photograph at Robertsbridge depicting the K. & S.R. train waiting for the main line train, seen here running in with DEMU set No 1012. The branch train is in fact a hop-pickers special for the K. & S.R., hauled by AIX No 32678, now preserved on the West Somerset Railway. The passenger service on the K. & E.S.R. was withdrawn in 1954.

The scene at Tenterden in B.R. days with the Tenterden goods ready to return to Robertsbridge in 1957. The engine is No 32678, now preserved.

The East Kent Railway in 1957 with an S.L.S. railtour behind 01 class No 31434, a reboilered South Eastern Railway 0-6-0, seen here at Eythorne—note the flat bottom non-B.R. track. The line has not been used since 1984 and may not reopen.

Last day scenes on the Hawkhurst branch on 12 June 1961 with C class 0-6-0 No 31588 at Cranbrook, the picturesque station between Hawkhurst and Goudhurst which still exists as a private house. The site is very overgrown and unrecognizable today. In the lower picture the single line token is being exchanged.

The last train to run over the Hawkhurst branch was on 20 June 1961 when a "clearing up train" traversed the branch.

Hawkhurst Station, in the lower picture, with goods shed, gantry, signal, and water tower, in the summer of 1961, a month before closure—the signal box still exists.

Crossing trains at Lydd Town on the New Romney branch with H class 0-4-4T left and class 2, 2-6-2T No 84020 right.

New Romney & Littlestone-on-Sea, showing the exterior of the building in the mid-fifties. The line closed to passengers and freight on 6 March 1967.

Dungeness platform with the famous lighthouse in the rear. Passenger services ceased on 4 July 1937 and freight in May 1953.

The Folkestone Harbour branch in steam days was quite spectacular, with trains being worked by up to four locomotives on this steeply graded 1 in 30 incline. In the upper picture, two R1 class 0-6-0 tanks work the empty "Golden Arrow" stock. In the lower shot, the ex-G.W.R. pannier banks an up train at East Cliffe Crossing in 1961.

Triple-headed trains were quite the norm on the Folkestone Harbour branch before electrification. In the upper picture, three R1 class 0-6-0s approach Folkestone Junction, and in the lower, a member of the same class gives the "Golden Arrow" empties a shove in May 1956.

Bexhill West with H class No 31520 about to start out for Crowhurst with the branch railmotor in March 1957 (lower picture), and a general view of the spacious South Eastern & Chatham Railway's terminal of 1902.

CROWHURST TO BEXHILL WEST

This branch was opened by the S.E. & C.R. on 1 June 1902, giving a much shorter journey to passengers to London of 62 miles as against 78 via the L.B. & S.C.R. route. The line was closed during World War I from 1 January 1917 and reopened on 1 March 1919. The station buildings at Bexhill were on a grand scale and the exterior facade was in a fine late-Victorian style. The branch was dieselised in June 1958 but closed completely on 15 June 1964. Had the main line from Tunbridge Wells to Hastings been electrified in 1961 with the rest of the South Eastern Division lines, the branch may have survived.

TUNBRIDGE WELLS WEST TO GROOMBRIDGE & ERIDGE

Tunbridge Wells West closed to all traffic on 12 August 1985, the passenger service Eridge to Tunbridge Wells West having ceased on 8 July 1985 and the Tunbridge Wells Central station being renamed Tunbridge Wells as from 30 September 1985. The station at Tunbridge Wells Central has been renovated for the complete Hastings line electrification (1986) and was rebuilt by the S.E. & C.R. in 1911. Tunbridge Wells West station, loco shed of four roads, goods yard and signal boxes are empty and awaiting the developer's bulldozers. There is a preservation scheme for the line to Eridge but so far the money has not been forthcoming, and the land is valuable and likely to be developed. Tunbridge Wells West was in fact the L.B. & S.C.R. terminal in town with services from Eastbourne, Tonbridge, Brighton, East Grinstead, and even Victoria. The L.B. & S.C.R. had a district office situated above the booking hall and the station was one of the focal points of the system. Tunbridge Wells West was still gas lit at the cessation of services in 1985, one of the last gas-lit stations on B.R.

TUNBRIDGE WELLS TO EAST GRINSTEAD

East Grinstead to Tunbridge Wells opened on 1 October 1866, the intermediate stations were at Forest Row, Hartfield, Withyham and Groombridge—the line was later to cross the line from Oxted to Eridge, constructed at a later date. The East Grinstead to Ashurst Junction section closed to all traffic on 2 January 1967. The connecting line, Ashurst Junction to Groombridge closed to all traffic on 6 January 1969. Forest Row station was removed after closure but Hartfield and Withyham are still intact and in a fine state of repair, having been sold by B.R.—the former in use for commercial purposes and the latter as a private house. Today the line is walkable from Groombridge to East Grinstead; the footpath is known as "The Forest Way". The section in the cutting at East Grinstead has been turned into a road bypass of the A22, known as "Beeching Way", named after a local resident.

TUNBRIDGE WELLS TO LEWES

There was an hourly service from Tonbridge to Brighton in B.R. steam days, usually worked by Tonbridge locomotives—these could be anything from an elderly Wainwright D class 4-4-0 to a Maunsell Mogul. Tunbridge Wells West to Lewes was the second line to open from Tunbridge Wells, the line through Eridge and Uckfield opening for business on 3 August 1868. The section from Uckfield to Lewes had been opened on 18 October 1858, the line from the Lewes end having originally left Lewes off of the main London line facing northwards. The line was opened as the Lewes & Uckfield Railway and in 1864 the L.B. & S.C.R. purchased it. The old spur from the Uckfield line facing towards Lewes from the main line was put out of use with the Tunbridge Wells opening of 3 August 1868. The abandoned line can still be seen, although mainly overgrown. Today Uckfield is a "branch" from Hurst Green Junction, the Uckfield to Lewes section having been closed to all traffic on 24 February 1969. In the summer of 1984, a new private railway was opened at Isfield and runs for a short distance along the old trackbed towards Uckfield. The "Lavender Line", as it is known, already has three locomotives, including a North British 2-10-0 from Greece, four coaches and a steam crane. Steam trains are run and are free, although there is an entrance fee to the site, and the station has been carefully restored to Southern Railway colours. Things move pretty rapidly nowadays—this must be the quickest preserved railway.

TUNBRIDGE WELLS TO EASTBOURNE

The line from Eridge to Polegate via Heathfield closed to all traffic by 9 September 1968, the section from Heathfield to Hailsham having closed on 26 April 1968. The passenger service over the whole line and the freight service from Eridge to Heathfield was closed on 14 June 1965. This line was known locally as the "Cuckoo Line" and had all its ex-L.B. & S.C.R. stations intact at the time of passenger closure. The "Brighton" preferred subways to footbridges and used a lot of timber in the building and framework. A feature of some "Brighton" country stations was the platform signal frame usually provided by the Southern so that the station could be one-man operated. Hailsham to Eridge (Redgate Mill Junction) was opened on 1 September 1880, and the Polegate to Hailsham section opened on 14 May 1849. The section from Heathfield to Hailsham is now a public footpath, "The Cuckoo Walk", and is being extended another three miles to Polegate.

The Oxted to Eridge section of double-track "main line" was opened from Hurst Green Junction to Edenbridge on 2 January 1888 and Edenbridge (Town) to Eridge on 1 October 1888. Thus the Eridge triangle was complete by 1888. This formed an alternative through route from London to Brighton via Oxted and Uckfield. Today the line is merely the "main" line Uckfield to Hurst Green Junction and, as there are no plans for electrification, could probably close when East Grinstead is electrified in 1987.

LEWES TO SEAFORD

The first railway in the area was the L.B. & S.C.R. line to Newhaven Harbour, opened on 8 December 1847 from Lewes. The L.B. & S.C.R. were keen to get a share of the continental traffic in competition with the South Eastern Railway via Folkestone. The extension from Newhaven on to Seaford was opened on 1 June 1864 and the line was electrified on 1 July 1935. A feature of train working on the line was the operation of the Newhaven boat trains, especially in steam days. When this had to be done, relief trains in the summer were worked by the L.B. & S.C.R. H2 class 4-4-2s until the class was withdrawn in 1958. The normal boat trains were worked in post-war years by the S.R. electric locomotives BR 20001 series, known to railway staff as "Hornbys" on account of their appearance. A visit to Newhaven shed in 1955—56 would be very rewarding as all the locomotives on shed would be of ex-L.B. & S.C.R. origin—K 2-6-0s, E4 0-6-2s, AIX 0-6-0s, and of course H2 4-4-2s.

LEWES TO EAST GRINSTEAD (CULVER JUNCTION–EAST GRINSTEAD)

The last train ran from East Grinstead to Lewes on 16 March 1958, hauled by a standard class 4 2-6-4 No 80154 built at Brighton—in fact the last engine to be built there. The Bluebell saga became well known as B.R. closed the line on 29 May 1955 instead of the proposed 13 June 1955. This was because of the ASLEF strike, but a local resident pointed out that the line had been closed illegally because an act of Parliament was required to close the line. B.R. had to reopen the line until the necessary legal proceedings had been dealt with; so the line reopened in 1956 only to close again in 1958. But all was not lost, for the line opened again on 7 August 1960 between Horsted Keynes and Sheffield Park as the Bluebell Railway—this was the first preserved standard gauge railway and as a result the line has inherited some really old locomotives including two L.B. & S.C.R. AIX class 0-6-0s. The saga may not yet be complete, for the Bluebell are pressing for an extension to East Grinstead, that is reopening the original line through Kingscote and West Hoathly. The process will be very lengthy, as land has to be re-purchased from individuals who bought it from B.R. after the 1956 closure. In the original act, Barcombe and Kingscote stations were not mentioned so they were not reopened in the 1956 reopening. The line was opened by the L.B. & S.C.R. in 1882 and proved to be a useful diversionary route to the London to Brighton main line. The Bluebell has now become an established institution, visited every year by day trippers and tourists. The line has featured many times in films, TV ads and plays, and everybody recognises the railway the instant that it flickers onto the TV screen.

HAYWARDS HEATH TO ARDINGLY

This line connected with the Bluebell at Horsted Keynes, a remote junction in the depths of Sussex. The line was electrified in 1935, the trains originating from Seaford. The service was intended to run to East Grinstead as an electrified through route but the 1939—1945 war stopped all that and Horsted Keynes was left high and dry as an odd backwater electric branch until closed on 28 March 1963 to all traffic. The L.B. & S.C.R. had opened the through route on 3 September 1883, the stub end of the branch to Ardingly A.R.C. Stone terminal is still in use. For modern day gricers wishing to sample the past, a visit to the refreshment room at Horsted Keynes can transport the passenger back in time.

THREE BRIDGES TO EAST GRINSTEAD

This line was the first railway to East Grinstead, opened on 9 July 1855 and terminating at the original East Grinstead (which can still be seen), before the High Level and extensions east and south were completed. There were two intermediate stations on the line—one at Grange Road and the other at Rowfant. The line was dieselised after 1965 and survived until 2 January 1967 when it was closed to all traffic. The line is now a public footpath and bridleway known as the "Worth Way". The High Level at East Grinstead was dismantled in 1970. East Grinstead Low Level is the station still in use today on the present line from South Croydon which is to be electrified in 1987. But this may not be good news, as this may coincide with the closure of the Uckfield line.

HORSHAM TO GUILDFORD

The single track line from Christs Hospital to Guildford (Peasmarsh Junction) was opened throughout on 2 October 1865; there were intermediate stations at Slinfold, Rudgwick, Baynards, Cranleigh and Bramley. Christs Hospital as a station was not opened until 28 April 1902, with the re-siting of the school of that name. The branch was just outside the suburban area and retained a rural appearance about it right up until closure on 14 June 1965—had the line been electrified, it would still probably be open. The trackbed is now a public footpath and bridleway, the stations having been demolished except Baynards, which has been restored to its original condition by its owner—a devoted enthusiast. The remains of the platforms at Bramley can still be seen beneath the undergrowth; the S.R. concrete nameboard is still in position—Bramley & Wonersh. Closure of this line could have been a short-sighted policy as new housing estates have sprung up along the course of the old trackbed. The distance from Horsham to Guildford was 19½ miles. Most of the route of this former branch is now a footpath known as "The Downs Link".

HORSHAM TO SHOREHAM (ITCHINGFIELD JUNCTION – SHOREHAM)

The Steyning line was opened throughout on 16 September 1861 from Shoreham to Itchingfield Junction. The distance from Horsham to Shoreham was 20 miles and there were intermediate stations at Bramber, Steyning, Henfield, Partridge Green, West Grinstead and Southwater. The line was double track throughout and regarded by the L.B. & S.C.R. more as an alternative route to the coast rather than a branch line. The line escaped electrification by the Southern Railway in the 1930s and was not planned to be electrified by B.R. after 1948—as a result, the old L.B. & C.R. steam classes could be seen at work. From Brighton or Horsham sheds D3 class 0-4-4s gave way to M7 class 0-4-4s which in turn gave way to L.M.R. class 2 2-6-2s. The line was eventually dieselised in May 1964; M7 class 0-4-4 tanks were never popular with Central Division loco crews and did not last very long in the area. The line was closed to all traffic on 7 March 1966 except for the Shoreham to Beeding section which was retained for the cement works—this closed on 1 May 1980. Parts of the line have been built on, and most of the trackbed has now been turned into a public footpath known as the "Downs Link" except for the part at Steyning which is now the A283 Steyning bypass.

THE DYKE BRANCH

This was an unusual line of 3½ miles which left the main line at Aldrington Halt which was at sea level and climbed up onto the South Downs to 400ft. The line was opened on 1 September 1887 and catered for day trippers from Brighton. Worked by the L.B. & S.C.R., the line was closed from 1 January 1917 to 26 July 1920, like so many minor lines during that period. The line terminated short of the summit which left passengers another 200ft climb. With the advent of the motorbus, the line's patronage declined. The branch was worked by E4 class 0-6-2s at closure which took place on 1 September 1939.

KEMP TOWN

This 1½ mile long suburban line was opened on 2 August 1869. The journey from Kemp Town to Brighton station took 10 minutes and season ticket holders on the main line could travel the branch for no extra charge. The line became operated by push & pull trains and was closed temporarily from 1 January 1917 to 1 September 1919. Closure to regular passenger trains took effect from 2 January 1933 but freight train operation lasted much longer and eventually ceased on 28 June 1971. A special service was arranged by B.R. on Saturday, 26 June 1971—an hourly service ran between 1000 and 2100, fares were 25 pence for adults and 15 pence for children, although the last train leaving at 2100 cost 50 pence.

RAILWAYS TO MIDHURST

Midhurst was the centre for three lines, one from Pulborough, one from Chichester, and the third from Petersfield—the former two were L.B. & S.C.R. owned whilst the latter was of L. & S.W.R. origin. Prior to the 1923 grouping, the L. & S.W.R. had its own terminal at Midhurst, and this station closed on 12 July 1925. The first railway to Midhurst was opened on 15 October 1866 from Pulborough, with stations at Fittleworth, Petworth and Selham. The Petersfield line, with intermediate stations at Rogate and Elsted, was opened on 1 September 1864 and worked by the L. & S.W.R. The last line to be built to Midhurst was the Chichester branch, opened on 11 July 1881 with stations at Havant, Singleton and Cocking. This line passed through rural, sparsely populated countryside and was uneconomic, closing to passengers on 6 July 1935. The section of the line from Midhurst to Cocking closed after the branch goods fell down an embankment on 19 November 1951 near Midhurst, the line having been washed away in a flood. The C2X class 0-6-0 that had worked the train (32522) was retrieved on 25 February 1952—a special ramp had to be laid in to tow the engine back onto the track. The locomotive was repaired at Brighton works and lasted another ten years in service. The truncated line beyond Havant to Cocking and Singleton closed to all traffic on 31 August 1953. The Lavant to Chichester part of the line is still in use with gravel being shifted in bulk trains from Lavant to Drayton for concrete making. The stations on the line still survive—one of them, Singleton, is now the Chilsdown Vineyard. All services on the Petersfield to Midhurst line ceased on 7 February 1955, and passenger services for Midhurst to Pulborough ceased on the same day. Freight traffic ceased from Midhurst to Petworth on 12 October 1964, and Petworth to Pulborough on 23 May 1966.

MISCELLANEOUS LINES

The L.B. & S.C.R. did have lines to Bognor Regis, opened 1 June 1864, and Littlehampton, opened 16 March 1846, but as these "branches" have a through service to London, Brighton and Portsmouth, they cannot be counted as branch lines in the true sense. Chichester was where the West Sussex Railway or Hundred of Manhood & Selsey Tramway commenced. The line was 7½ miles long and opened in 1897 as a light railway and was part of the Colonel Stephens empire, closing to all traffic on 19 January 1935. The line was not taken over by the Southern Railway and closed too early to be part of the Southern Region. Had the line survived until 1948, it would have probably been nationalised and disposed of quickly, as was the East Kent Light Railway. The short 1½ mile branch of the former South Eastern Railway from Rye to Rye Harbour closed on 29 February 1960—this was a goods only line. Part of the line is now a road.

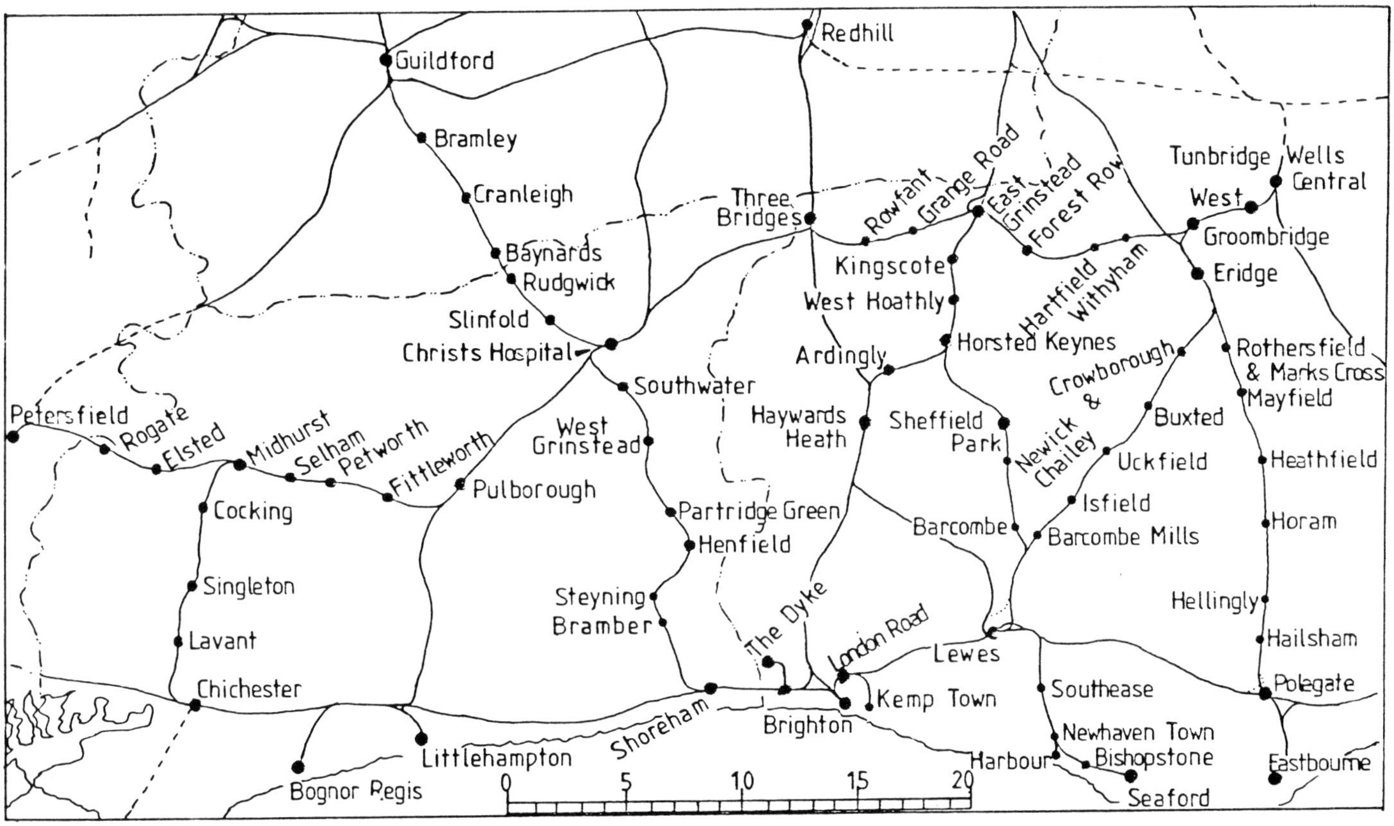

Rowfant on the Three Bridges to East Grinstead line, with S.E. & C.R. H class 0-4-4T No 31530 propelling. The trains were push and pull worked—note the platform ladders used for access to the oil lamps. The station still exists, although very overgrown, with the trackbed now a footpath.

Horstead Keynes the day befo
the East Grinstead to Lew
service was withdrawn—the co
ductor rails serve the Haywar
Heath line—15 March 1958.

Sheffield Park on the last day
operation on 16 March 195
with class 4 2-6-4T en route
Lewes. The site has now great
changed—the siding is now a
engine shed.

Ardingly, showing the spacious L.B. & S.C.R. station with 4 BIL stock running in on a Haywards Heath to Ardingly train. This service was withdrawn to passengers on 28 March 1963. The station buildings at Ardingly still exist and have been turned into offices of the A.R.C. who still use the line for stone trains.

West Hoathly, on the last weekend of operation, sees an East Grinstead to Lewes train with a B.R. standard class 4 2-6-4T. The station buildings have been demolished and the track lifted—only the trees remain on the left. This line will eventually see trains again, as the Bluebell Extension Railway.

Tunbridge Wells West is no more, having closed to all traffic on 12 August 1985. Here, H class No 31519 prepares to depart for Tonbridge with S.E. & C.R. stock.

Isfield sees the 4.50p.m. Victoria to Brighton accelerating away for Lewes with H2 class 4-4-2 No 32424 "Beachy Head" in August 1953. This classic shot is by Syd Nash.

Heathfield, with class 4 2-6-4T No 80013 working a Tunbridge Wells West to Eastbourne train in March 1964. The passenger service on the line was withdrawn on 14 June 1965. Today, the trackbed from Heathfield to Polegate is open as a public walk known as the "Cuckoo Way".

Eridge, with an Eastbourne to Tunbridge Wells West train clanking out behind class 4 2-6-4T No 80084 in March 1964.

The Dyke branch closed down completely on 1 September 1939. The line was used by Sentinel steam railcars for a brief perioc in the 1930s, but these took a very limited load and had to be transferred elsewhere.

The Kemp Town goods continued to run for many years after the passenger service ceased in 1937. In the picture below, E4 class 0-6-2T shunts the sidings in April 1962. Right, the last day was celebrated on 26 June 1971 by B.R. with an hourly service throughout the day.

Last trains to Kemptow

Saturday 26 June 1971

Trains will run every hour between Brighton and Kemptown from 10.00 to 21.00

Journey takes 10 minutes

RETURN FARE

25p Adult 15p Children (3 and under 14)

SPECIAL LAST TRAIN

Leaving Brighton 2100

50p Return fare (no reduction for children)

You can post a letter in a specially designed commemorative envelope at a small extra charge

DISPLAY AT BRIGHTON STATIO OF 'EVENING STAR'

the last steam locomotive built by British Rail

Admission 10p

Details and reservations from:
Mr. D. K. Plummer, Assistant Station Manager, Brighton station BN1 3XP
or telephone Brighton 26211 Ext. 7388

ALL PROCEEDS WILL BE DONATED TO THE SOUTHERN RAILWAYMEN'S WOKING HOMES

Bramley & Wonersh on the Guildford to Horsham line presents a placid scene in this 1959 photograph and shows plenty of detail for the modeller. the crossing gates can be seen with their interlocking to keep them shut, operated from the "Brighton" box, and various other pieces of equipment including the concrete nameboards which still exist.

Christ's Hospital, shortly before closure in June 1965, with class 2 2-6-2T leaving for Guildford with the commodious branch platforms in the background.

Cranleigh with H class No 31279 arriving from Guildford in August 1959. Note the Southern Railway "shunt ahead" signal, left, mounted on an old L.B. & S.C.R. post.

Baynards, with Ivatt class 2 2-6-2T No 41294 leaving for Guildford. Note the engineers' wooden structure gauge leaning against the goods shed wall. This would be used for checking clearances on the nearby tunnel. Wonder of wonders, this station still exists and has been restored to its original L.B. & S.C.R. colours.

Steyning, with class 2 2-6-2T No 41260 leaving for Brighton on what is now the town bypass, A283.

Southwater, with 80152, one of the last of the class 4 2-6-4Ts to be built at Brighton. The trackbed is now a footpath known as the "Downs Link". The line closed to all traffic on 7 March, 1966.

Scenes on the Midhurst goods on 14 April 1960. Above, the three days a week goods stops at the then picturesque Fittleworth, now in a terrible state of decay and overgrown with trees. Left, E4 class 0-6-2T No 32469 shunts at Petworth. The station is now fully restored as a private dwelling.

Lavant in 1959, showin the fine L.B. & S.C.R. timber architecture and very high platform to take sugar bee trains. Today, the line is stil used from Lavant to Chichester by aggregate trains.

FARNHAM TO ASH JUNCTION (Surrey)

The short length of line from Farnham to Ash Junction of nearly 3 miles in length had two stations, one at Tongham and the other at Ash Green. The service was from Farnham to Guildford, avoiding Aldershot. The passenger service was withdrawn on 4 July 1937 on the occasion of electrification of the Alton line from Woking. Freight services lasted from Tongham to Ash Junction until 2 January 1961. The track from Farnham Junction to Tongham was lifted in January 1955, the exact date of the cessation of freight trains being unclear.

BENTLEY TO BORDON

This line was opened on 11 December 1905 by the L. & S.W.R. and was a light railway being 4½ miles long. The line was built to connect with the Longmoor Military Railway at Bordon, opened at about the same time. The Longmoor Military had access to its own system from both Bordon and Liss, the L.M.R. having a considerable system where army engineers, usually ex-railway staff, were trained. The Longmoor Military had workshops, engine sheds, breakdown cranes and a large garrison. Locomotives and rolling stock were secondhand from the main line railways and the system was very busy during both wars. The platforms at Bordon were sufficiently lengthy to contain troop train movements. The Bordon to Bentley branch was worked by L.S.W.R. M7 class 0-4-4s but closed to passengers on 16 September 1957. Freight traffic ceased on 4 April 1966 and the Longmoor Military closed on 31 October 1969. Some rolling stock survived and the most famous of the Longmoor engines, the 2-10-0 "Gordon" of Rev. Awdry fame, can be seen at Bridgnorth on the Severn Valley. A feature of the Bordon to Bentley branch was the halt at Kingsley where the L. & S.W.R. planted trees to give some shelter to waiting passengers. The L. & S.W.R. favoured poplars, unlike the all too common G.W.R. pine.

ALTON TO BASINGSTOKE

The Basingstoke & Alton Light Railway had a chequered career and a certain amount of fame but little remains to be seen of this interesting line today. The 12½ mile line was opened by the L. & S.W.R. in 1901 and closed on 30 December 1916 as a wartime economy measure. The Southern Railway reluctantly reopened the line on 18 August 1924 and closed it again on 12 September 1932. The railway had been put there in the first place mainly to keep the G.W.R. from encroaching on L. & S.W.R. territory. The Southern Railway did hire the line out to film companies, the most spectacular film being *The Wrecker* made in 1928 which featured a South Eastern Railway 4-4-0 No A148 being crashed. The Southern Railway did the thing in style, the *Southern Railway Magazine* reporting the matter in great detail. A special train left Waterloo at 6.30a.m. on Sunday, 19 August 1928 with dining cars full of press photographers and reporters, breakfast was served on the train which terminated at Herriard. The crash was staged at Salters Ash Crossing where the loco No A148 (F1 class) plus 6 coaches was crashed into a stationary Foden steam lorry. A large marquee was erected in the field overlooking the crossing, even tickets were issued to visitors to see the show at Lasham Hill Farm. The line was used again for filming purposes in June 1937 when *Oh! Mr. Porter* was filmed at Cliddesden—one of the most famous of railway films. The Basingstoke & Alton was lifted shortly afterwards but the numberplates and worksplate of "Northiam", one of the locomotives used, are still in existence and are at the National Railway Museum.

ALTON TO WINCHESTER

Alton to Alresford is now open to regular passenger trains, being part of the preserved Watercress Railway—a distance of 10½ miles. The Watercress (Mid Hants Railway) commenced services into Alton from Medstead on 25 May 1985, the track having been reinstated on 12 April 1985. The line reopened in parts: the section from Ropley to Medstead on 28 May 1983, and the section Alresford to Ropley on 30 April 1977. The line has a good selection of motive power to greet the visitor, including Bulleid pacifics, Maunsell moguls, standard BR classes, and an L. & S.W.R. T9 4-4-0. The gradients are fairly tough, so big engines are required to work the trains. The line originally closed on 5 February 1973 from Winchester Junction to Alton, and the section Winchester Junction to Alresford has now had the track lifted.

HURSTBOURNE TO FULLERTON JUNCTION

This short connecting line from Hurstbourne on the main West of England line was opened on 1 June 1885 to Fullerton Junction on the L. & S.W.R. Andover Junction to Romsey branch. The line was built as a double track line with the intention of keeping the G.W.R. out of Southampton, as a spur was planned and even partially built from the G.W.R., Newbury to Winchester line near Whitchurch. The intermediate stations were at Longparish and Wherwell and were intact when the line closed completely on 28 May 1956. The Hurstbourne to Longparish section was closed to all traffic in 1934, the passenger service ceasing on 6 July 1931. Longparish and Wherwell stations still exist and are in use as private residences.

BROCKENHURST–WEST MOORS–CHRISTCHURCH

This was the original route to Christchurch and Bournemouth prior to the opening of the more direct main line through New Milton. The original line to Christchurch went via Ringwood and Hurn and lasted until 30 September 1935, the line having been opened on 13 November 1862. The Brockenhurst, Ringwood, Dorchester main line was opened on 1 June 1847. The route from Brockenhurst to Broadstone Junction was useful to the Southern when running diversions avoiding Bournemouth. In the summer timetable certain Waterloo to Weymouth trains ran via Ringwood on Saturdays. The standard service, usually M7 class 0-4-4s on push & pull sets, was Bournemouth West to Brockenhurst in BR days. The line closed to all traffic on 4 May 1964 from Brockenhurst to Ringwood, and on 7 August 1967 from Ringwood to West Moors. The original "main line" from Ringwood to Christchurch had one intermediate station at Hurn and, although this was closed in September 1935, the station at Hurn can still be visited as it is now the Avon Causeway Hotel (free house). The track was lifted in 1937. There are proposals to convert the sections between Ringwood and West Moors and between Ringwood and Brockenhurst to footpaths, some parts of the latter section being already open to the public.

ANDOVER JUNCTION TO ROMSEY

The Andover and Redbridge Railway opened on 6 March 1865 enabling connection with the main line through to Southampton. The railway was built independently and was built on the course of the Andover canal. The L. & S.W.R. acquired the Andover & Redbridge and extended the line from Andover Town to Andover Junction on the main line. The Midland & South Western Junction Railway connected with the L. & S.W.R. at Andover Junction, and as a result through services ran from the north of England to Southampton. The through services continued up until closure of the M. & S.W.J.R. until 11 September 1961 when that line was closed as a through route. There were through trains from Cheltenham to Southampton and Southern region engines worked them right through to Cheltenham. Andover Junction to Romsey closed to passengers on 7 September 1964, the Andover Town to Romsey (Kimbridge Junction) closed to all traffic on the same date but the section from Andover Town to Andover Junction lasted until 18 September 1967.

The loss of the through route from the north was the primary cause of the Andover to Romsey line's eclipse. The line was dieselised in 1958, prior to which it was worked by T9 class 4-4-0s of L. & S.W.R. origin. Romsey to Eastleigh via Chandlers Ford still has one daily passenger train. There are proposals to convert Andover to Romsey into a continuous footpath, some parts being already public footpaths or highways.

ALTON TO FAREHAM (MEON VALLEY RAILWAY)

The Meon Valley line, 22¼ miles in length, was opened on 1 June 1903 by the L. & S.W.R. and was intended as an alternative main line to Fareham and Portsmouth. The line was opened fairly late for a main line, for the L. & S.W.R. were wary of the G.W.R who always had ambitions to expand to the coast in the Solent area. There were stations at Tisted, Privett, West Meon, Droxford, and Wickham—some of these stations still exist, having been turned into private houses. Halts were opened at Farringdon (1931) and Knowle (1907). The station buildings were unusual in that they had sliding doors on the platform entrance from the booking hall. A peculiarity of the route was the section opened in 1904 by the L. & S.W.R. who built a double track deviation line from Knowle Junction into Fareham around Knowle tunnel. The single track section through Knowle tunnel was still used by Meon Valley trains until closure. The passenger service was withdrawn on 7 February 1955 and the section from Droxford to Farringdon closed to all traffic on the same day. The stub end of the line from Farringdon to Alton survived until 5 August 1968. At the bottom end of the line services ceased for all traffic from Knowle Junction to Droxford on 30 April 1962. The station at Droxford was used for the HQ of the Allied Expeditionary Force in 1944 where the Prime Minister's train was stabled in the sidings. A framed photograph of Churchill and Eisenhower used to hang in the booking hall at Droxford. The Meon Valley line was railtoured on 6 February 1955 by an RCTS special headed by two T9 class 4-4-0s Nos 30301 and 30732. The Meon Valley was worked by many of the L. & S.W.R. locomotive types at closure including M7 class 0-4-4 tanks on the push & pull, 700 class 0-6-0s on the goods, and T9 class 4-4-0s on the occasional through train. Today, Tisted, Privett and Droxford survive as private houses—Tisted and Privett having been beautifully restored. West Meon has been razed to the ground, but the track bed from there to Knowle Junction is now a public footpath.

There was a short but abortive attempt at preservation on the Meon Valley. Mr. Charles Ashby bought Droxford station and used the track to test the Sadler Pacerailer railbus during the 1960s. The line also had AIX No 32646 which was stored at Droxford until 1966 when it was sent to Hayling Island to be mounted outside a pub. The AIX is now at Haven Street on the Isle of Wight. The Southern Loco Preservation Co. bought a diesel shunter and U.S.A. tank No 30064 in 1969, and 30072—another U.S.A. tank. The S.L.P. Co. moved to Liss, then packed up, and eventually No 30064 ended up on the Bluebell and 30072 on the Keighley & Worth Valley.

BISHOPS WALTHAM

This short 3½ mile branch from Botley was opened on 6 June 1863 as the Bishops Waltham Railway, being purchased by the L. & S.W.R. in 1864. Passenger services ceased at an early date on 2 January 1933 but the daily goods lasted until 30 April 1962, when the line was closed completely. There was one intermediate halt at Durley opened in 1909 for the L. & S.W.R. railmotor service.

THE SOUTHSEA RAILWAY (EAST SOUTHSEA BRANCH)

This was a 1½ mile long line from Fratton to Southsea opened on 2 July 1885 and was jointly owned by the L.B. & S.C.R. and the L. & S.W.R. The line was worked by railmotors and closed on 8 August 1914 as a wartime economy measure and never reopened.

GOSPORT AND LEE-ON-SOLENT

The Gosport branch was one of the L. & S.W.R.s oldest lines—in fact the line was opened as a main line terminal on 29 November 1841, being a branch of the London & Southampton Railway from Eastleigh (then called Bishopstoke). The line gave access to Portsmouth and Gosport had a superb colonnade, but after the opening of Portsmouth Harbour, Gosport station declined in importance. The branch did have royal patronage in that Queen Victoria used the line to Clarence Pier, which was an extension of Gosport, on her way to the Isle of Wight. The passenger service to Gosport from Fareham ceased on 8 June 1953. The section from Bedenham to Gosport station closed to all traffic on 6 January 1969. The Fareham to Gosport line had a branch to Stokes Bay from Gosport Junction just outside Gosport station. The Stokes Bay line and pier were opened on 6 April 1863, worked by the L. & S.W.R. and sold to the Admiralty on 3 March 1922. The purpose of the line to Stokes Bay was to give a shorter sea crossing to the Isle of Wight, but the regular passenger service finished on 1 November 1915. The Admiralty took over the pier during World War I and used it for torpedo research. After the 1922 purchase, the Stokes Bay line was lifted and sold to the local authority but the pier is still there today. The Lee-on-Solent Light Railway opened in 1894 from Fort Brockhurst—an intermediate station on the Gosport branch. Freight services ceased on 29 September 1935 and passenger services on 1 January 1931. The section Fareham to Bedenham near Gosport is still used by the Navy but Stokes Bay and Fort Brockhurst are now public footpaths. The L. & S.W.R. used ex-L.B. & S.C.R. AIX class 0-6-0s on the railmotor to Lee-on-Solent and Bishops Waltham—the engines were purchased by the L. & S.W.R. in 1903 and numbered 734 and 735. No 734 ex-L.B. & S.C.R. No 46 survived until November 1963, having worked the Hayling Island branch until closure. The locomotive which had worked on the Isle of Wight was mounted on a plinth outside a pub at Hayling—fortunately the engine was purchased and returned to the Isle of Wight in 1979 and has now been restored to Southern livery.

HAYLING ISLAND

This line was famous for the use of ex-L.B. & S.C.R. AIX class 0-6-0 tanks which worked it until closure to all traffic on 4 November 1963. AIX classes had to work the line because of the weak wooden bridge at Langstone. In the summer, the Havant to Hayling Island branch had a service of four trains per hour, all AIX worked. Two of the AIXs are on the K. & E.S.R., Bluebell, and Isle of Wight respectively—this includes the oldest survivors which date from 1872. Hayling Island to North Hayling is now a footpath.

TOTTON, HYTHE & FAWLEY LIGHT RAILWAY

This was one of the lines built by the Southern Railway after grouping and was opened on 20 July 1925. The line was single track throughout with stations at Hythe and Fawley, and the distance was 9 miles. The passenger service was sparse and considered secondary to the freight traffic which was to the oil refinery at Fawley, opened by Esso. Passenger services were withdrawn on 14 February 1966. The line is still very much in use today for, apart from the oil traffic, there are other industrial sidings on the line.

BROCKENHURST TO LYMINGTON PIER

The branch to Lymington was opened on 12 July 1858 to Lymington Town, the Pier section being opened on 1 May 1884. The line is still thriving, having been electrified in July 1967, the present multiple units having replaced the ageing M7 class 0-4-4 tanks and push and pull units of Maunsell origin.

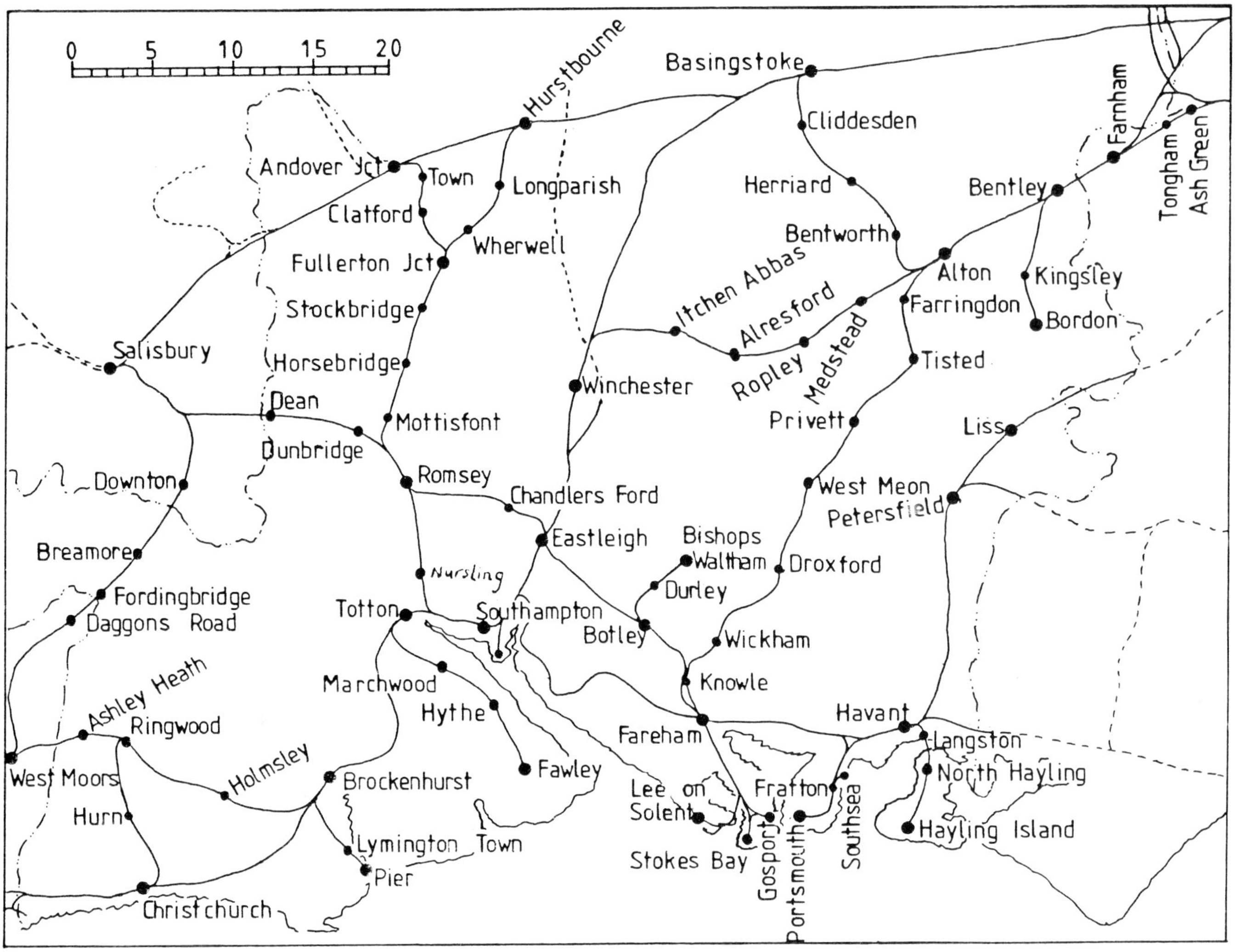

Ropley, on the Mid Hants Railway in Southern Railway days, with a T1 class 0-4-4T arriving. The immaculate topiary has been restored and the present-day loco shed is situated in the goods yard behind the loco.

Maunsell mogul No 31808 leaves Fullerton with a Southampton bound stopping train hauling B.R. standard passenger stock in the old B.R. red and cream colours. The engine had started out life as one of the famous river K class 2-6-4 tanks of 1926, having been converted to a U class 2-6-0 in 1928 and finally being withdrawn in 1961.

Fullerton, with the Longparish goods in August 1955—the locomotive is an L.&S.W.R. 700 class 0-6-0. The line closed to goods in May 1956.

Droxford Station on the Meon Valley Railway, which closed to passenger trains in 1955, with an M7 class 0-4-4T in 1959 on a B.L.S. railtour.

Droxford today, in use as a private house and scene of the experiments with the Pacerailer railbus during the 1960s.

Bishops Waltham, with the daily goods in 1958; the passenger service was withdrawn in 1933 by the S.R., although the goods lasted until 30 April 1962.

Lymington Pier in steam days sees an M7 class 0-4-4T pushing a Maunsell push and pull set towards the boats. This branch still thrives, having been electrified in 1967.

Fawley sees some parcels traffic in March 1958 with M7 class 0-4-4T No 30033. The line was one of the Southern's pre-war openings, having been opened in July 1925. Passenger services were withdrawn in 1966 although the line is still open for oil. Fort Brockhurst, junction for the former Lee-on-Solent branch which was closed to all traffic on 29 September 1935, sees a railtour organised by the Branch Line Society in March 1959. The train was going to Gosport—note the L. & S.W.R. gas lamp on the left.

Bordon, towards the buffer stops. The station had lengthy platforms to accommodate troop trains for the nearby Longmoor Military Railway. The station closed on 16 September 1957.

Holmsley, a fine example of L. & S.W.R. country station, on the old main line from Brockenhurst to Wimborne, with M7 class 0-4-4T No 30108. Note the L. & S.W.R. clerestory roofed signalbox on the platform. This line is now partly a public footpath.

Scenes on the Hayling Island branch in 1963 with AIX class 0-6-0T No 32650, in the upper picture, seen approaching Hayling North—unusual for a Southern Halt, as it was of timber construction. In the lower picture, the same engine is being coaled at Hayling Island. This locomotive, formerly No 50 "Whitechapel" of the L.B. & S.C.R. and built in 1876, still works today on the Kent & East Sussex Railway.

The Isle of Wight system was one of the great attractions in steam days as all the locomotives and rolling stock dated from pre-grouping companies. Generally speaking, the locomotives were L. & S.W.R. and L.B. & S.C.R., O2, E1 and AIX, whilst the rolling stock was S.E. & C.R. or L.B. & S.C.R. This situation arose as a result of the rolling stock from suburban steam lines, electrified during the 1920s, being transferred to the Isle of Wight. Some of the pre-1923 rolling stock has survived, as has the O2 class 0-4-4 tank and two AIX class 0-6-0s, now kept at the Isle of Wight Steam Railway at Haven Street. The Isle of Wight system was grouped into the Southern Railway in 1923. The Island had three constituent companies: the Isle of Wight Railway, from Ryde to Ventnor including the Bembridge branch; the Isle of Wight Central, from Ryde to Cowes, with Ventnor Town and Newport to Sandown branches; and the Freshwater, Yarmouth and Newport Railway. In addition to these three concerns, the section of main line from Ryde Pier Head to St. Johns Road was jointly owned by the L. & S.W.R. and the L.B. & S.C.R. All of the Island was steam worked until 31 December 1966 when the remaining part of the system from Ryde Pier Head to Shanklin was electrified with secondhand LT stock from the Bakerloo Line.

The first closures on the Island were the Ventnor West line on 15 September 1952, the Bembridge and Freshwater lines on 21 September 1953, and the Newport to Sandown line on 6 February 1956, all to all traffic. The next closures were the Ryde (Smallbrook Junction) to Cowes section on 21 February 1966 to passengers, and the Ventnor to Shanklin line on 18 April 1966 to all traffic. Freight traffic held on from Medina Wharf to Cowes until 16 May 1966, and Medina to Smallbrook Junction until 24 October 1966. The first railway on the Island was the Cowes and Newport Railway, being opened on 16 June 1862. There was no doubt that the railways on the Island had a character of their own. The Southern painted all the engines green, named all of them and kept them spotlessly clean. The engines had Caledonian hooters and the trains were air-braked, the locomotives were fitted with the Westinghouse pump. The countryside was unspoilt and the branch lines little used. The present Isle of Wight Steam Railway gives a good impression of travel on the system 30 years ago. Some parts of the Isle of Wight system are now in use as footpaths.

Southern Railway publicity of the 1920s showed the high spots of the Island's tourist attractions as well as a reference to the Southern's three constituents.

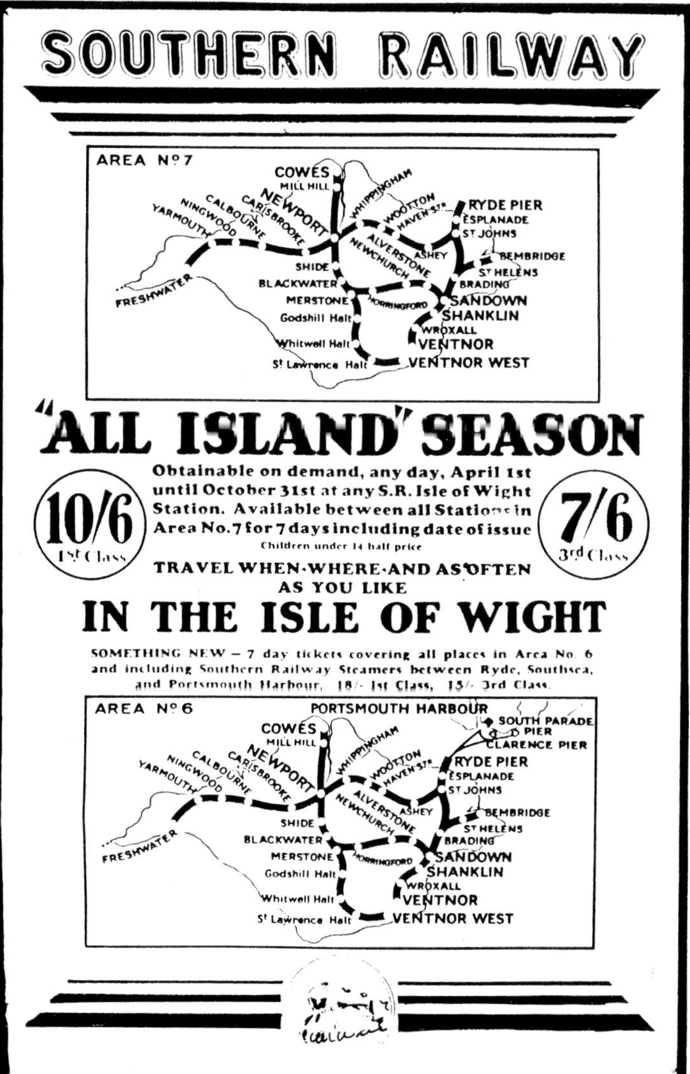

Last day at Ventnor West, with the station staff and loco crew gathered around No 27 "Merstone", built in 1890 and shipped to the Island in 1926. Note the stove next door to the water column to prevent the water freezing up in winter.

Ventnor West, looking towards the buffer stops, with worn bull head rail and wooden keys. This former Isle of Wight Central Railway terminus closed to all traffic on 15 September 1952.

Yarmouth, on the Freshwater branch, a few days before closure which took place on 21 September 1953. The station site is now a housing estate but the trackbed from Yarmouth to Freshwater is now a footpath.

Ryde St. Johns Road, with the works in the rear, sees 02 class No 17 and L.B. & S.C. stock in July 1966. The Adams 02 0-4-4T No 17 "Seaview", was built at Nine Elms in 1891 and brought to the Isle of Wight in 1930.

Shanklin, with Ventnor bound train hauled by 02 0-4-4T No 26 "Whitwell", and Southern starting signal mounted on old rails. Photograph taken in August 1958 when the line had a 15-minute service.

Cowes, in the heyday of the line in the summer of 1959, with 02, 0-4-4T No 16 "Ventnor" of 1892 in the upper picture, and Cowes (lower) a few years after closure in 1966 with the vegetation taking over.

Ryde St. Johns Road, with No 17 "Seaview" and the loco shed in the background in the upper picture, and No 28 "Ashey" of 1890 charging the bank out of Ryde with S.E. & C.R. stock in July 1966 in the lower.

No 24 "Calbourne" belts uphill out of Ryde in the summer of 1958 with L.B. & S.C. stock on the double track section to Smallbrook Junction. No 24 is the sole survivor of the Island 02s and can now be seen at Haven Street on the preserved Isle of Wight Steam Railway.

Freshwater, the terminu of the former Freshwate Newport & Yarmout Railway, with 02 cla No 33 "Bembridge". Th line closed to all traff on 21 September 1953

Shed scene at Newport with 02 class No 25 "Godshill" of 1890 protruding out of the ironwork. Note B.R. square restricted clearance plate on shed wall.

A1 class 0-6-0T No 12 at Newport in Southern Railway days—formerly No 84 "Crowborough" of 1880; this was the last terrier to be built and was withdrawn as No 12 "Ventnor" in 1936. The engine languished until 1949 when it was cut up at Eastleigh.

Bembridge, with AIX No 9 "Fishbourne" now at work on the K. & E.S.R. as No 10 "Sutton"—formerly No 50 "Whitechapel" of 1876.

BULFORD CAMP

The L. & S.W.R. opened the 8-mile long branch to Bulford from Idmiston to Amesbury on 29 April 1902, and Bulford on 1 June 1906. The line was built primarily for the military traffic on Salisbury Plain. There was a direct connection off the branch facing Salisbury to Porton which was opened on 7 August 1904. The branch had 10 trains per day in June 1914, but by 1952 this had been reduced to one train per day. The line closed to passengers on 30 June 1952 and freight on 4 March 1963, the last train being a railtour organised by the Railway Enthusiasts Club, of Farnborough fame, on 23 March 1963. The train was a push & pull unit hauled by M7 class 0-4-4 No 30108. The direct connection from Amesbury Junction to Newton Tony Junction closed to all traffic on 30 June 1952, the same day that the passenger service was withdrawn.

SALISBURY TO WEST MOORS (ALDERBURY JUNCTION–WEST MOORS)

The Salisbury to West Moors line opened on 20 December 1866 and was independent until bought by the L. & S.W.R. in 1883. The line was secondary to the more direct route but was useful as a diversionary line to Bournemouth. There was always a through train from Waterloo to Weymouth by this route, being a split off the overnight newspaper train. This 24-mile long line also had its fair share of long-distance holiday trains on summer Saturdays in the post-war period. Passenger traffic to seaside resorts grew to enormous sizes during the period 1945 to 1960, the peak being reached in 1958. Bournemouth and Poole were one of the favourite places and trains would come from all over the country on Saturdays in the summer. The line closed to all traffic on 4 May 1964. All of the five intermediate stations were excellent examples of L. & S.W.R. architecture and were in Southern Railway colours. L. & S.W.R. signalling survived until closure and so did some of the L. & S.W.R. enamel nameboards on the stations. West Moors to Wimborne is now a road—the 5½-mile Ferndown bypass.

HAMWORTHY AND BOURNEMOUTH WEST

The Hamworthy branch opened on 1 June 1847, the station being known as Poole. The line closed to passengers on 1 July 1896, but today is still open to freight, there being a cement terminal and coal depot. The line has at times been visited by various railtours since 1896.

The Bournemouth West terminus was opened on 15 June 1874 and became part of the L. & S.W.R. This was the terminus for the ill-fated Somerset & Dorsest Railway trains. Summer Saturday trains in the years prior to the S. & D. closure came from Derby, Bradford, Sheffield, Manchester, Bristol, Birmingham and Nottingham—these were all through trains. Bournemouth West station closed to passengers on 4 October 1965 and the station site has now been redeveloped in connection with a new road scheme.

SWANAGE

The Swanage branch was opened on 20 May 1885 by the L. & S.W.R., being 11 miles from Wareham. The line closed completely on 2 January 1972, the section from Worget Junction to Furzbrook being retained for oil trains, this being a newly discovered oil-producing area of Britain. At the other end of the former Swanage branch is The Swanage Railway Company, another fast-growing private railway, which runs trains for the public from Swanage to Heston—a short distance of approximately 1¼ miles. The Swanage Railway wish to extend their line to Hormans Cross and, eventually, Corfe Castle, although a bypass is proposed which makes extension difficult. The actual track at present extends for 2 miles from Swanage to New Barn Bridge.

PORTLAND & EASTON

The branch to Portland was opened on 16 October 1865 and was jointly owned with the G.W.R., becoming Southern Region after 1948. The line was extended to Easton, being jointly owned between the G.W.R. and the L. & S.W.R., and opened on 1 September 1902. Easton to Melcombe Regis (Weymouth) closed on 3 March 1952 to passengers, and freight from 5 April 1965. The present Weymouth Quay line was formerly G.W.R. owned, still runs through the streets, and conveys passengers to the Channel Island ships.

YEOVIL TOWN TO YEOVIL JUNCTION

Yeovil Junction to Yeovil Town was opened by the L. & S.W.R. on 1 June 1861, the station at Yeovil Town being jointly owned with the G.W.R. The distance from Yeovil Junction of 1¾ miles was worked in Southern days by an M7 class 0-4-4 and a push & pull unit—the train was known locally as the "Bunk". The passenger service was withdrawn on 3 October 1966 and the town station closed—it is now a car park.

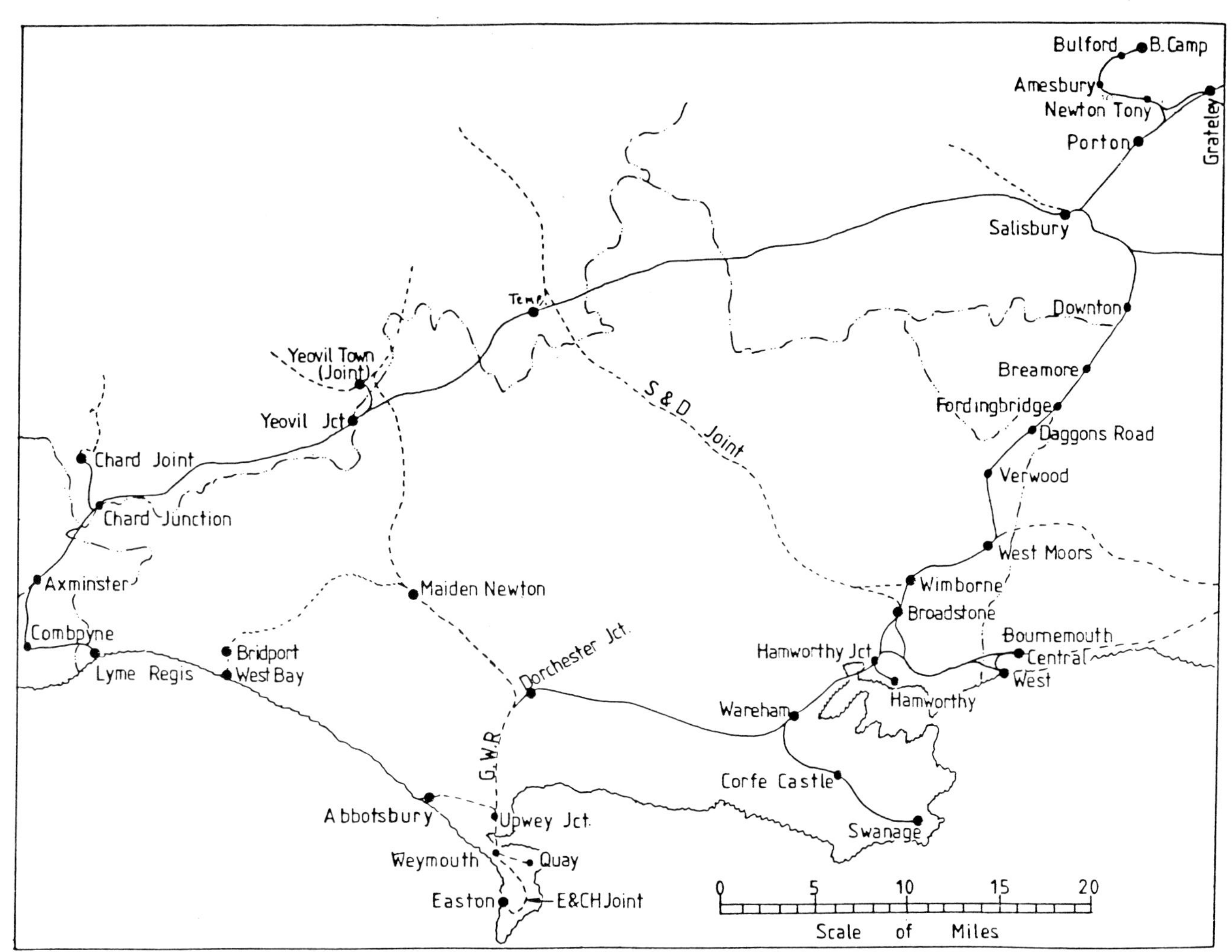

BRANCH LINES IN WILTSHIRE, SOMERSET & DORSET (Continued)

CHARD JUNCTION TO CHARD TOWN

The 3¼-mile line from Chard Junction to Chard was opened on 8 May 1863. The L. & S.W.R. had a station at Chard Town but when the Bristol & Exeter Railway arrived on the scene on 11 September 1866 a new joint station was opened, with broad gauge from Taunton on one platform and standard gauge from Chard Junction on the other. The L. & S.W.R. terminus at Chard Town was closed on 30 December 1916 and the line worked entirely by the G.W.R. to Chard Junction. The Chard Joint Station was renamed Chard Central by B.R. in 1949, and the G.W.R. branch became part of the Southern Region from 2 April 1950. This was later returned to the Western Region probably in 1958. Chard Junction to Chard Central closed to all traffic on 30 October 1966, the G.W.R. branch from Taunton (Creech Junction) having closed to all traffic on 6 July 1964 and the passenger service Chard Junction to Town having been withdrawn on 10 September 1962. A feature of the Chard Central station layout was the long interchange platform for transhipment of goods between the standard and broad gauge—this could be seen until closure in 1966.

AXMINSTER TO LYME REGIS

The Axminster & Lyme Regis Light Railway was 6¾ miles long and opened as late as 24 August 1903. There was only one intermediate station at Compyne, near Cannington Viaduct, which was the principal engineering feature of the line. The viaduct had to be reinforced shortly after opening in 1903 as the land subsided and a mini-arch had to be put in the third arch. The viaduct can still be seen and is made of concrete. The L. & S.W.R. used AIX class 0-6-0s to start with, then O2 class 0-4-4s but these were superseded by the well-known Adams 4-4-2 tanks which worked the line until the 1960s. One of these engines survives as No 488 (built 1885) on the Bluebell Railway, Sussex. The locomotive also worked on the ill-fated East Kent Railway. The Adams 4-4-2 locomotives lasted until 1960 when they were replaced by Ivatt 2-6-2s of L.M.R. design. The line eventually became dieselised and closed to all traffic on 29 November 1965. A feature of train operation was that on summer Saturdays during the post-war period, through trains were run to Lyme Regis from Waterloo. For this operation, the trains were double headed with the Adams 4-4-2 tanks. The severe curvature of the track guaranteed the survival of the Adams tanks until track improvements were carried out in 1960 for the Ivatt class 2, 2-6-2s. There are proposals by Devon County Council to turn the trackbed into a public footpath.

Bulford—M7 class No 30108 arrives with an R.E.C. special in March 1963. The Bulford branch had a sparse service and closed to passengers on 30 June 1952 and freight on 4 March 1963. This was the last train.

Breamore (Hants)—a study of a London & South Western country station. The station is still in Southern Railway colours in this 1962 photograph.

Fordingbridge (Hants), on the Salisbury to West Moors line, with L. & S.W.R. nameboard, signalbox and platform barrows. The station has a commodious goods yard and even still has the wartime white paint stripes on the waiting shelter in this 1962 photograph.

Wimborne—crossing trains with class 4 2-6-0 No 76028 on a Bournemouth to Salisbury stopping train. An example of this class can be seen on the Mid Hants Railway.

Corfe Castle, with M7 class wheezing past one of the ruins that Cromwell "knocked about a bit". It is the ambition of the present Swanage system to extend to this point.

Yeovil Junction on the main line with M7 class 0-4-4T No 30129 waiting for a connection.

Yeovil Junction to Yeovil Town, with M7 class 0-4-4T No 30129 near Yeovil town propelling the "bunk" with Maunsell stock. The passenger service was withdrawn on 3 October 1966 and the Town station is now a car park.

Swanage, looking very much as it is today, but with Bulleid passenger stock berthed and M7 class 0-4-4T ready for departure to Wareham.

Lyme Regis, with Adams 4-4-2T No 30582 in the pouring rain in January 1961. This engine, one of three dating from the 1880s, only lasted another six months, being withdrawn in July 1961. One example survives as No 488 on the Bluebell Railway.

SEATON TO SEATON JUNCTION

The Seaton branch of 4½ miles was opened on 16 March 1868 as the Seaton & Beer Railway, which was later bought by the L. & S.W.R. There were two stations on the line at Colyton and Colyford. The line in post-war years was worked by L. & S.W.R. M7 class 0-4-4 tanks and railmotor sets until their displacement by panniers and G.W.R. 14XX class 0-4-2s. The line became Western Region on 1 January 1963. The branch closed to all traffic on 7 March 1966 but that was not the end of the Seaton branch. In September 1969, the tramway at Eastbourne closed and was packed up and relaid on the trackbed of the Seaton B.R. branch. The Seaton Tramway, as it is known, was opened on 28 August 1970 to Colyford. The 2 ft 9 in gauge electric tramway was extended to Colyton in 1977, and operates during the summer season, the tramcars being ⅔rds scale of a standard gauge version. The line reopened is 3 miles long and terminates by the old L. & S.W.R. station at Colyton—the section onto what was Seaton Junction having been lifted by B.R.

RAILWAYS TO EXMOUTH & SIDMOUTH

The line from Sidmouth Junction to Sidmouth opened on 6 July 1874 as the Sidmouth Railway. The connecting line from Tipton St. Johns to Exmouth via Budleigh Salterton opened throughout on 1 June 1903. The Sidmouth Railway was worked by the L. & S.W.R. and remained independent until 1922. The Sidmouth branch closed to passengers on 6 March 1967, the same day as the Exmouth to Tipton St. Johns section. Freight finished to Sidmouth on 8 May 1967 from Sidmouth Junction. Sidmouth Junction station reopened on 3 May 1971 as Feniton. The section from Tipton St. Johns to Exmouth closed to all traffic on 6 March 1967. Today only the direct line to Exmouth from Exeter (Exmouth Junction), opened on 6 March 1861, is still in use. An unusual working, prior to the closure of the Somerset & Dorset line in 1966, was the through train from Exmouth and Sidmouth to Cleethorpes. This train ran on summer Saturdays only and joined up at Tipton prior to reversal onto the main line at Sidmouth Junction. Trains were run between holiday resorts, as many people had a week in each resort.

BARNSTAPLE TO ILFRACOMBE

The 15 miles from Barnstaple Junction to Ilfracombe could be classified as a branch line, or the end of the line from Waterloo. Ilfracombe, being 226 miles 16 chains from Waterloo, had a through service. The through services from Waterloo to Devon and Cornwall were legendary and the trains could consist of nine portions for nine destinations. Ilfracombe could end up with one coach from Barnstaple Junction in the winter, the load being an easy one for a West Country class pacific. The line opened on 20 July 1874 and included some stiff gradients—1 in 40 up to Mortehoe, and 1 in 36 down into Ilfracombe over a 2¼-mile length which necessitated freight trains being banked. The Ilfracombe line even had an all-Pullman service which commenced on 20 June 1947. The train, the "Devon Belle", left Waterloo at 12 noon, ran non-stop to Wilton where there was an engine change, and split at Exeter, one part going to Ilfracombe and the other part going to Plymouth. The train lasted until 1954, a feature being the observation cars, one of which can now be seen on the Dart Valley Railway. The line closed on 5 October 1970 to regular passenger trains and was not lifted until 1975, the last train being an engineers saloon on 26 February 1975. There was a proposal to preserve the railway, the North Devon Railway Society being inaugurated in 1971. A company was floated but nothing came of it, so B.R. sold off the parts of the line that it could. Braunton to Barnstaple is now a public footpath, and so is Ilfracombe to Mortehoe. Further proposals for footpaths include Braunton to Mortehoe and Barnstaple Junction to Bideford.

LYNTON & BARNSTAPLE RAILWAY

Much has been written about the Southern's 2 ft gauge railway and the way in which it was rapidly closed down on 30 September 1935, the line being lifted shortly afterwards. Regrettably the line, which nowadays would have considerable tourist potential, was treated by its owner purely on a cost basis. The Southern Railway were very cost-conscious and if they had a bad case they simply hacked a branch off. The railway opened on 11 May 1898, ran through fine countryside, possessed some excellent Manning Wardle 2-6-2 tanks and was missed by all those who were lucky enough to see it. There are one or two relics still to be seen, including the original terminus at Lynton (now a house), Woody Bay station (also now a house), and Bratton Fleming station (now a pub). The viaduct at Chelfam still exists as well. The *North Devon Herald Journal* of 24 December 1985 reported that the Lynton & Barnstaple Railway Association wanted to reopen the line. The opening proposals state that there is no intention of reopening the Barnstaple section, that the line would run in the summer only, would be run by volunteers and could not gain access to Lynton owing to street congestion. Well, if Ropley to Alton can be relaid to a standard gauge, then a Lynton & Barnstaple should be easier! Today, nothing is impossible, especially with railway preservation. The bay platform at Barnstaple Town station can still be seen at the derelict station site.

TORRINGTON TO HALWILL (North Devon & Cornwall Junction Light Railway)

The extension southwards from Torrington had been planned by the L. & S.W.R. but World War I and the railway grouping delayed opening until 27 July 1925 by the Southern Railway. The engineer in charge was the redoubtable Colonel H.F. Stephens, the line being constructed to the standard gauge utilising the 6½ miles of the 3ft Torrington & Marland. The line was dual gauge until opening in 1925 over the Torrington and Marland section, and was 20 miles long when complete. Passenger traffic was sparse, the Southern used E1/R class locomotives—these were Stroudley E1 class 0-6-0 tanks rebuilt for use in the area with larger bunkers and an extra trailing wheel. The E1/R class were ousted eventually by Ivatt class 2, 2-6-2 tanks in the mid-fifties—these in turn gave way to a single unit railcar in the sixties. The passenger service from Torrington to Halwill finished on 1 March 1965, the portion of the line below Meeth was also closed to all traffic and lifted in 1966. Meeth goods was officially closed on 16 October 1982, the last run being in August 1982. Passenger services from Torrington to Barnstaple ceased on 4 October 1965, but there were specials and railtours after that, including Joannes specials for enthusiasts, day trippers and Christmas shoppers to Paddington. The last train to Torrington from Barnstaple was organised by B.R., ran on 6 November 1982 and originated from Bristol. The stations have been turned over to a variety of uses—Torrington is now a restaurant, Bideford is a branch of the Midland Bank, and Instow a marina office.

HALWILL TO BUDE

The line from Okehampton to Bude was opened on 20 January 1879 to Holsworthy, the extension to Bude being opened by the L. & S.W.R. on 10 August 1898. The 18½ mile line from Bude included stations at Whitstone, Holsworthy and Dunsland Cross. The services on the line included the through coaches to Waterloo on the multi-portioned Atlantic Coast Express which left Waterloo at 11.00a.m. and arrived at Bude at 4.12p.m. This train, which ran in nine portions, would on summer Saturdays be split into two trains, one serving North Devon and the other servicing North Cornwall. Closure of the Bude branch took place with effect from 3 October 1966 to all traffic. The stations were still very much in their original condition—Whitstone & Bridgerule still had the original L. & S.W.R. black and white enamel nameboards at closure in 1966.

HALWILL TO PADSTOW

The North Cornwall Railway, as this outpost of the L. & S.W.R. was known to railway staff, closed to all traffic between Wadebridge and Meldon Junction on 3 October 1966—the same day as the Bude line closure. Padstow had through services to Waterloo by way of the Atlantic Coast Express, the line having been completed to Padstow on 27 March 1899. The distance between Padstow and Halwill was 49¾ miles with 11 intermediate stations. At Launceston the line made connection with the G.W.R. branch from Plymouth, which closed to all traffic on 28 February 1966. There is now a narrow gauge railway at Launceston, open in the summer to tourists. The line is 2ft gauge, approximately 1 mile long and worked by two locomotives from Penryn and Dinorwic—both are Hunslets of 1883 and 1898, and the line is on the B.R. track bed.

BODMIN & WADEBRIDGE

The Bodmin & Wadebridge Railway opened on 4 July 1834 and was one of the earliest railways in the West of England—the distance from Bodmin North to Wadebridge being 6¾ miles. The connecting line from Bodmin General to Boscarne Junction was built by the G.W.R. and opened in 1887, this resulted in the curious layout at Bodmin whereby the L. & S.W.R. and the G.W.R. had their own stations in the town (Bodmin North and Bodmin General in B.R. days). G.W.R. trains would work through from Bodmin Road to Wadebridge via Bodmin General—Bodmin Road is now renamed Bodmin Parkway. The Bodmin & Wadebridge was eventually absorbed into the L. & S.W.R. after that company had reached Wadebridge via the North Cornwall line. Bodmin North to Dunmere Junction closed to all traffic on 30 January 1967, as also did the Wadebridge to Padstow line. Wadebridge to Boscarne Junction closed to all traffic on 5 September 1978 but the last train ran on 17 December 1978—a charter by Bodmin Lions from Bodmin Road to Wadebridge and back twice. The closure of Wadebridge and Bodmin North left the Wenford Bridge china clay line isolated as a mineral branch from Bodmin Road to Wenford via Bodmin General and Boscarne Junction.

WENFORD & RUTHERN BRIDGE

The branch from Wadebridge (Grogley Junction) to Ruthern Bridge was a mineral-only line and was closed by the Southern Railway on 30 December 1933, the last train being on 29 November 1933. This branch, like the neighbouring Wenford Bridge, opened as early as 30 September 1834, being part of the Bodmin & Wadebridge Railway. Both the Wenford and Ruthern lines were mineral lines only. The Wenford Bridge line was well known for the Beattie well tanks of L. & S.W.R. fame—two of these 2-4-0s survive as preserved museum pieces. The Wenford Bridge to Bodmin Road china clay line survived until 29 August 1985, and since then the North Cornwall District Council have made an offer to purchase the line from Boscarne Junction to Bodmin Parkway (Road) and negotiations are at present under way. The Wenford to Boscarne Junction section was lifted in September 1985 and it is proposed to relay it as a 2ft gauge line.

BERE ALSTON TO CALLINGTON

The present Gunnislake line to Plymouth was once the Callington branch to Bere Alston and then from there onwards the line was the L. & S.W.R. ex main line from Exeter to Plymouth. The Gunnislake branch is kept at present as it affords access from one side of the river Tamar to the other. The top end of the line from Gunnislake to Callington closed to all traffic on 7 November 1966. The former main line of the L. & S.W.R. from Bere Alston to Meldon closed to all traffic on 6 May 1968, the section from Bere Alston to Victoria Road (Plymouth) having been singled.

The Callington line started out as The East Cornwall Mineral Railway and was 3ft 6in in gauge running to Calstock Quay. The line was opened on 7 May 1872 and not extended to Bere Alston until 2 March 1908, where it joined the main line. The railway became the Plymouth, Devonport & South Western Junction Light Railway and was converted to standard gauge throughout. The main line from Lydford to Devonport Junction was P.D. & S.W.J.R. but was leased to and operated as part of the L. & S.W.R. main line.

BRANCH LINES AT PLYMOUTH

The L. & S.W.R. had a passenger terminal at Plymouth Friary and Southern trains to London started from here until rationalisation in the area brought about closure to passenger traffic on 15 September 1958. The present Southern Friary branch is still open for goods, as is also the Aberthaw Cement Terminal. The Cattewater line is open for oil trains, and the Plymstock line open for cement trains. The Plymstock line, originally going to Turnchapel, closed to passengers on 10 September 1951 and freight on 20 October 1961. The L. & S.W.R. branch from Devonport Kings Road to Stonehouse Pool closed to all traffic on 30 May 1970.

BARNSTAPLE TO TORRINGTON

This line had an interesting history in that part of it was broad gauge opening to Bideford on 2 November 1855. The L. & S.W.R. appeared on the scene and laid standard gauge to Bideford on 2 March 1863, the line being dual gauge from Exeter. The broad gauge lasted until April 1877. The L. & S.W.R. extended 5½ miles onwards from Bideford to Torrington on 18 July 1872—this was known as the Torrington Extension Railway. China clay was being excavated by the North Devon Clay Co. at Meeth and a 3ft gauge railway, the Torrington & Marland Railway, was constructed in 1880 and conveyed clay over the 6½ miles to Torrington where it joined the L. & S.W.R. The Torrington & Marland Railway was opened for mineral traffic only on 1 January 1881. The narrow gauge line lasted until it was replaced by the standard gauge Torrington to Halwill line in 1925.

Seaton terminus in July 1962 with M7 class 0-4-4T No 30125 of 1911. The branch closed in March 1966 but still functions partly as an electric tramway.

Colyford, with waiting passengers and ex-L. & S.W.R. M7 arriving in 1957. This site is now occupied by the Seaton Tramway, an electric tramway of 2ft 9in gauge formerly in use at Eastbourne.

Tipton St. John's still retains its L. & S.W.R. black on white enamel nameboard in this early B.R. shot with M7 and L. & S.W.R. stock. Sidmouth, always a cramped terminus, could boast a through service from Waterloo in its heyday. The short branch closed to all raffic on 8 May 1967.

Topsham, on the Exmouth to Exeter branch, which is still in use, shown here in April 1957. A fine unspoilt L. & S.W.R. country station with curious valancing to the canopy and a row of L. & S.W.R. barrows.

Littleham, in 1957, with an Adams 02 class 0-4-4T crossing an Exmouth bound train of L. & S.W.R. stock and Ivatt 2-6-2T. The signal is an L. & S.W.R. starter and the lengthman is just about to take his daily walk of inspection along the track, as prescribed in the rule book.

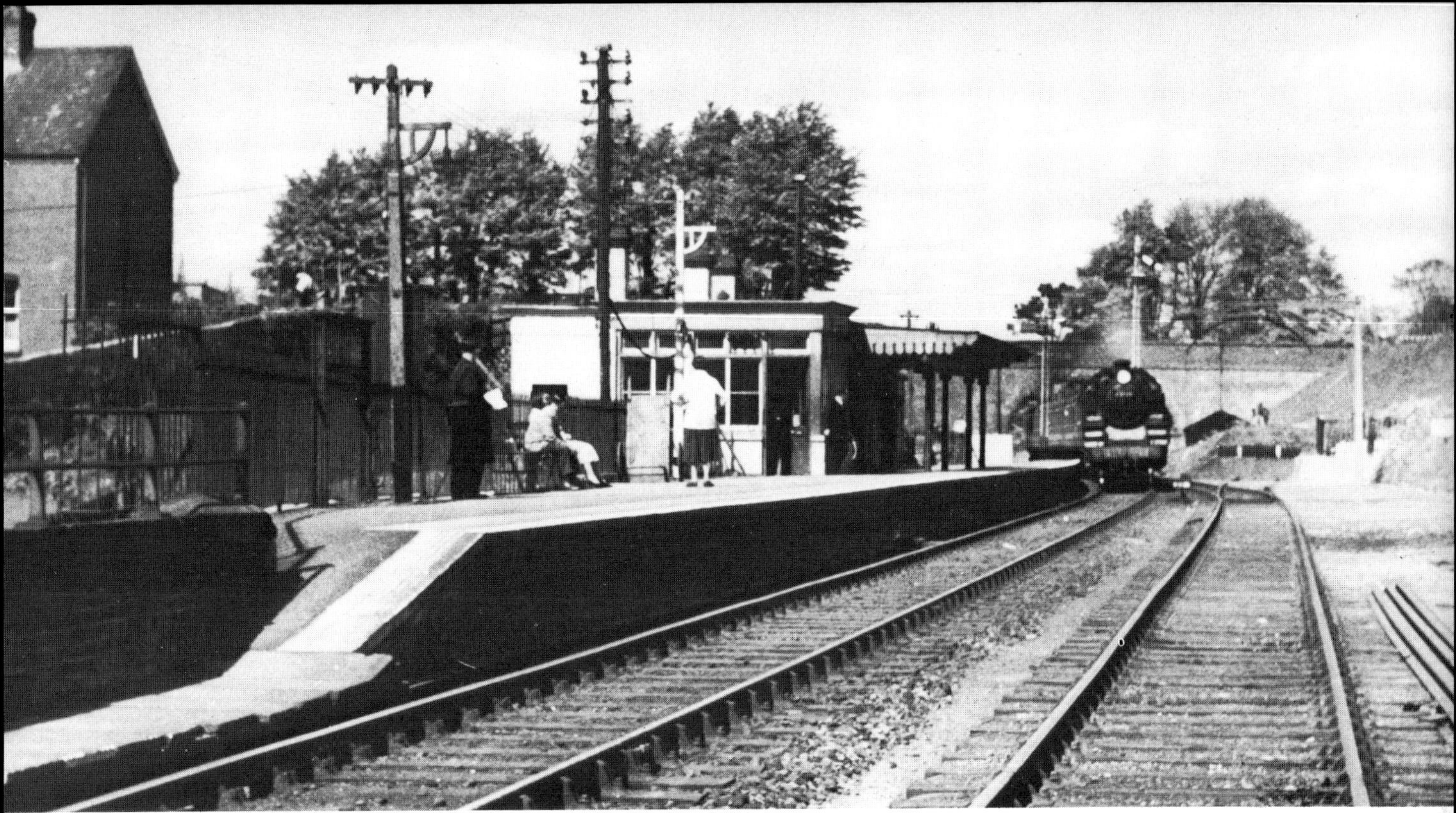

Lympstone sees a B.R. class 3 2-6-2T arriving with a train of B.R. standard stock. This class of engine was fairly rare, there being no preserved example. Note the L. & S.W.R. signals.

Turnchapel, an outpost of the Southern system, with a few standard concrete embellishments and S.R. shunt signal. The line was closed to passengers on 10 September 1951.

The spartan station accommodation at Turnchapel, above, with station building sited on the inside of the curve; and intermediate station at Oreston, below, with concrete posts for lighting.The line closed to passengers on 10 September 1951 and freight on 2 October 1961.

Callington — class 2 2-6-2T No 41302 about to start with branch train for Bere Alston in the rain on 2 November 1958. The station had an overall roof and closed on 7 November 1966 to Gunnislake to all traffic. Note the all wooden L. & S.W.R. starting signal.

Southern Railway No 756 0-6-0T "A.S. Harris" started as part of the Plymouth, Devonport & South Western Junction Railway stock but ended its days shunting in the Brighton area. The locomotive was a Hawthorn Leslie of 1907. No 756 lasted into B.R. days and was eventually scrapped at Eastleigh in October 1951.

Scenes on the North Devon & Cornwall Junction Light Railway on 7 November 1959, with an Ivatt class 2-6-2T and Maunsell stock at Petrockstow above, and Hatherleigh below. The line was opened as late as 27 July 1925 by the Southern Railway, the engineer in charge being Colonel Stephens—this was one of his last lines.

Hatherleigh, with Ivatt class 2 2-6-2T No 41216 waiting time on a single coach train on 2 May 1964, only a year before closure on 1 March 1965.

Whitstone & Bridgerule still boasts an L. & S.W.R. black and white enamel nameboard in this May 1964 picture, with Ivatt class 2 2-6-2T bound for Bude. The line closed to all traffic on 3 October 1966.

Ivatt class 2 2-6-6T No 41283 scoots along from Torrington to Barnstaple on 3 May 1964 with G.W.R. stock in B.R. maroon.

Halwill sees T9 class No 30719 arriving with a North Cornwall train in November 1959.

Egloskerry, on the North Cornwall, with N class No 31842 drifting in with a Maunsell two coach set. Note signalman waiting with single line token.

The North Cornwall line ran through sparsely populated countryside from Halwill to Padstow, opened as late as 1899. The line closed to all traffic on 3 October 1966 from Wadebridge to Meldon Junction. In the upper picture, N class No 31849 can be seen with a lightweight freight at Otterham. In the lower picture, St. Kew Highway looks desolate. Note topiary on the platform.

The Beattie well tanks were kept by B.R. to work the Wenford Bridge line until December 1962, when they were replaced by pannier tanks. Built as long ago as 1874, the two locos illustrated have both been preserved. No 30587, seen shunting at Wadebridge in 1958, can now be seen at Quainton Road where it is restored as S.R. E 0314. No 30585, in the lower picture, is now owned by the National Railway Museum and is seen shunting in the pouring rain at Tresaret Siding on the Wenford Bridge line in 1958.

The Lynton & Barnstaple Railway closed in 1935 and quite a few relics can still be seen today, including two stations. The most noticeable engineering feature is the all-concrete Chelfham viaduct, seen here in 1964, ready made for preservation.

maps by M. Pain

Cover photographs:
Front—Baynards. Rear—Tunbridge Wells West.
Both by C.J. Gammell.

ACKNOWLEDGEMENTS

The author and publisher wishes to thank the following for the use of their photographs in this book.

Aston, J.H., page 5, page 17 lower, page 27 upper page 38 upper and page 59 lower.
British Rail, page 2.
Burgess, A., page 32 lower, page 66 lower, page 71 upper.
Coltas, J.A., page 71 cente, page 87 lower.
Daniels, G., page 34 upper, page 37 upper, page 39, page 41 upper.
Dench, L., page 50 lower.
Joannes, R., page 30 lower.
Langford, J., page 41 lower.
Lens of Sutton, page 14 upper, page 18, page 30 upper, page 32 centre, page 33 lower, page 34 lower, page 38 lower, page 38 middle, page 66 middle, page 68 lower, page 71 lower, page 83, page 85 lower, page 86.
Nash, S., page 48 lower.
National Railway Museum, page 50 upper.
Pamlin Prints, page 66 upper.
Squire, M., page 69 lower, page 67 upper.
Wilmshurst, E., page 36, page 40.
Rest by C.J. Gammell.

Thanks also due to D. Mercer for printing of negatives.

APPENDIX 1: SOUTHERN REGION LINES OF GREAT WESTERN ORIGIN

Today, the Southern Region includes several lines which were not of Southern Railway origin. There are also lines which closed as Southern Region lines but belonged to the G.W.R. Since 1948 regional boundaries have changed several times, the most noticeable being the Southern Railway lines west of Exeter. In 1950 all Southern lines became Western Region, but were still used by the Southern Region for operating purposes on the section west of Exeter. In 1958 Southern lines were transferred back to the Southern west of Exeter. This situation existed until 1 January 1963 when all Southern lines west of Wilton South were transferred back to the Western Region—this included the existing branch lines. To the visitor to the West of England, this could be confusing as some stations were painted chocolate and cream but had green nameboards, and vice versa. The regional colour schemes now abolished can still be seen on the Barnstaple line where some stations are still in Southern green.

G.W.R. lines affected, in addition to the S.R. lines west of Exeter, were Chard to Taunton and Yeovil to Taunton, closed to all traffic on 6 July 1964, and Yeovil to Castle Cary, Bridport (closed completely 5 May 1975), Abbotsbury (closed completely 1 December 1952), Newbury to Winchester (D.N.S.R. closed completely 10 August 1964), and Savernake to Andover Junction (closed completely 11 September 1961). The Andover Junction to Ludgershall Section is still retained for military purposes. In addition the lines Basingstoke to Reading and Westbury to Salisbury are of ex-G.W.R. origin but have at some time been Southern Region.

The Somerset & Dorset Railway, jointly owned by the Southern and the L.M.S., became Western Region above Templecombe and Southern below. As the line originated from the Midland & L. & S.W.R. prior to 1923, a wide variety of locomotive classes could be seen. The Somerset & Dorset closed down completely in 1966.

APPENDIX 2: LIGHT RAILWAYS ACT 1896

Towards the end of the nineteenth century, railway promoters were having difficulty in providing new lines to remote areas, where the costs were marginal but the railway to a small community was considered essential for the development of the area. In the pre-motor age it must be remembered that the horse and cart was the only alternative to the railway on inland transport if one discounts the even slower canals. In order to serve rural areas light railways were constructed at a cheaper rate than a full main line railway; this involved lightly laid track, minimum ballasting, no crossing gates or keeper and little or no signalling. In the case of most light railways, trains were worked on a line on the "one engine in steam" principle. Tunnels and heavy engineering works were also usually absent on light railways, as were staff at stations—and in some cases stations themselves. The system was successful until the diesel engined bus started to ply upgraded roads, and when the country bus was firmly established the light railway was doomed.

APPENDIX 3: FURTHER READING

There has been recently published a book entitled *Railway Rights of Way*, a survey of unused lines. This is a book detailing closed lines that can be walked or even driven over. The book is published by the Branch Line Society. This Society also have a regular journal entitled *Branch Line News*—this gives the up-to-date happenings on lines open and closed. The regular railway magazines also feature the occasional article on specific lines; *Steam Railway* has a regular feature of before and after photographs, usually of branch lines.

BIBLIOGRAPHY

Rail Atlas of Britain S.K. Baker O.P.C. 1980
Passengers No More G. Daniels & L. Dench Ian Allan 1980
Preserved Locomotives H.C. Casserley Ian Allan 1980
A Guide to Steam Railways of Great Britain Rev. W. Awdry & C. Cook Pelham 1979
B.R. Pregrouping Atlas W.P. Conolly Ian Allan 1958
Branch Line Index G.C. Lewthwaite B.L.S. 1971
L. & S.W.R. Locomotives 1873–1922 F. Burtt Ian Allan 1949
Locomotive History of S.E. & C.R. D.L. Bradley R.C.T.S. 1980
The Elham Valley Line Brian Hart W.S.P. 1984
The Meon Valley Railway R.A. Stone Kingfisher 1983
Lines to Torrington John Nicholas O.P.C. 1984
History of Southern Railway R.W. Kidner/D. Marshall Ian Allan 1963
William Stroudley, Craftsman of Steam H.J. Campbell Cornwall D. & C. 1968
The Axminster to Lyme Regis Railway E.J. Rose Kingfisher 1982
The London, Chatham & Dover Railway Adrian Gray Maresborough 1984

Railway Magazine, Railway World, Steam World and *Branch Line News.*
Also Oakwood Press paperbacks, various editions and publications by Peter Harding.

INDEX TO LINES

Line	Date Closed to Passengers	Former Company	Page
Addiscombe—Elmers End	—	SECR	9
Allhallows-on-Sea—Hoo Jcn—Grain	4.12.61	SECR/SR	23
Alton—Winchester	5.2.73	LSWR	55
Alton—Basingstoke	12.9.32	LSWR	55
Alton—Fareham	7.2.55	LSWR	56
Andover Jcn—Romsey	7.9.64	LSWR	56
Angerstein Wharf—	—	SECR	8
Barnstaple Jcn—Ilfracombe	5.10.70	LSWR	79
Barnstaple Jcn—Torrington	4.10.65	LSWR	81
Bembridge—Brading	21.9.53	IWR	65
Bexhill West—Crowhurst	15.6.64	SECR	42
Bishops Waltham—Botley	2.1.33	LSWR	57
Bisley Camp—Brookwood	21.7.52	LSWR	20
Bodmin—Padstow	30.1.67	LSWR	80
Bordon—Bentley	16.9.57	LSWR	55
Bournemouth West—Branksome	4.10.65	LSWR	72
Bricklayers Arms—Bricklayers Arms Jcn	1852	SECR	8
Broadstone—Brockenhurst	4.5.64	LSWR	56
Broadstone—Hamworthy Jcn	4.5.64	LSWR	56
Bromley North—Grove Park	—	SECR	9
Bude—Okehampton	3.10.66	LSWR	80
Bulford—Porton	30.6.52	LSWR	72
Callington—Gunnislake	7.11.66	PDSW	81
Canterbury West—Lyminge	2.12.40	SECR	26
Caterham & Tattenham—Purley	—	SECR	10
Chard Jcn—Chard Central	10.9.62	LSWR	73
Chessington South—Motspur Park	—	SR	19
Chichester—Midhurst	8.7.35	LBSC	44
Christchurch—Ringwood	30.9.35	LSWR	56
Christs Hospital—Guildford	14.6.65	LBSC	43
Christs Hospital—Shoreham	7.3.66	LBSC	44
Cowes—Newport—Smallbrook Jcn	21.2.66	IWCR	65
Crystal Palace—Nunhead	20.9.54	SECR	9
Deptford Wharf—New Cross Gate	—	LBSC	8
Dungeness—Lydd	4.7.37	SECR	25
Dyke—Aldrington Halt	1.1.39	LBSC	44
East Grinstead—Lewes	17.3.58	LBSC	43
East Grinstead—Ashurst Jcn	2.1.67	LBSC	42
East Grinstead—Three Bridges	2.1.67	LBSC	43
East Southsea—Fratton	8.8.14	LSWR/LBSC	55
Easton—Melcombe Regis	3.3.52	ECHJ	72
Epsom Downs—Sutton	—	LBSC	10
Eridge—Hailsham	14.6.65	LBSC	42
Exmouth—Sidmouth Jcn	6.3.67	LSWR	79
Farnham—Ash Jcn	4.7.37	LSWR	55
Fawley—Totton	14.2.66	SR	57
Folkestone Harbour—Folkestone Jcn	—	SECR	24
Freshwater—Newport	21.9.53	FYNR	65
Fullerton—Hurstbourne	6.7.31	LSWR	55
Gosport—Fareham	8.6.53	LSWR	57
Gravesend West—Farningham Road	3.8.53	SECR	23
Greenwich Park—Nunhead	1.1.17	SECR	8
Hailsham—Polegate	9.9.68	LBSC	42
Halwill—Torrington	1.3.65	LSWR	80
Halwill—Wadebridge	3.10.66	LSWR	80
Hampton Court—Surbiton	—	LSWR	19
Hamworthy—Poole	1896	LSWR	72
Hawkhurst—Paddock Wood	12.6.61	SECR	23
Hayes—Elmers End	—	SECR	9
Hayling Island—Havant	4.11.63	LBSC	57
Headcorn—Robertsbridge	4.1.54	KESR	25
Horsted Keynes—Haywards Heath	28.10.63	LBSC	43
Kemp Town—London Road	2.1.33	LBSC	44
Lee-on-Solent—Fort Brockhurst	1.1.31	LSWR	57
Lewes—Seaford	—	LBSC	43
Lewes—Uckfield	24.2.69	LBSC	42
Leysdown—Queenborough	4.12.50	SECR	24
Lyme Regis—Axminster	29.11.65	LSWR	73
Lyminge—Shorncliffe	16.6.47	SECR	26
Lyminton Pier—Lymington	—	LSWR	57
Lynton—Barnstaple	30.9.35	L&BR	79
Merton Park—Tooting	3.3.29	LBSC/LSWR	19
Necropolis—Brookwood	1.5.41	BNR	20
New Romney—Appledore	6.3.67	SECR	25
Newport—Sandown	6.2.56	IWCR	65
Padstow—Bodmin North	30.1.67	LSWR	80
Petersfield—Midhurst	7.2.55	LSWR	44
Pevensey—Polegate	30.8.68	LBSC	42
Plymouth—St. Budeaux V.R.	7.9.64	LSWR	81
Plymouth Friary—North Road	15.9.58	LSWR	81
Polegate—Hailsham	9.9.68	LBSC	42
Port Victoria—Grain	11.6.51	SECR	23
Pulborough—Midhurst	7.2.55	LBSC	44
Queenborough Pier—Queenborough	1.3.23	SECR	24
Ramsgate Harbour—Broadstairs	2.7.26	SECR	24
Ramsgate Town—Margate Sands	2.7.26	SECR	24
Salisbury—West Moors	4.5.64	LSWR	72
Sandgate—Hythe	1.4.31	SECR	26
Sandling—Hythe	3.12.51	SECR	26
Sandwich Road—Eastry	1.11.28	EKLR	25
Seaton—Seaton Jcn	7.3.66	LSWR	79
Sheerness—Sittingbourne	—	SECR	24
Shepherdswell—Wingham	1.11.48	EKLR	25
Shepperton—Strawberry Hill	—	LSWR	19
Sidmouth—Sidmouth Jcn	6.3.67	LSWR	79
Stoke Jcn Halt—Grain	4.12.61	SECR	23
Swanage—Wareham	3.1.72	LSWR	72
Tunbridge Wells West—Eridge	12.8.85	LBSC	42
Turnchapel—Plymouth Friary	10.9.51	LSWR	81
Ventnor—Shanklin	18.4.66	IWR	65
Ventnor West—Merstone	15.9.52	IWCR	65
Wenford—Boscarne Jcn	—	LSWR	80
West Croydon—Wimbledon	—	LBSC	19
Westerham—Dunton Green	30.10.61	SECR	23
Whitstable Harbour—Canterbury West	1.1.31	SECR	24
Wimbledon—Sutton	—	SR	19
Windsor & Eton—Staines	—	LSWR	20
Woodside—Selsdon	16.5.83	SE/LBSC	9
Yeovil Town—Yeovil Jcn	3.10.66	LSWR	72